MW01124784

FOR
MERCY

LESSONS I WOULD HAVE
TAUGHT MY DAUGHTER

ALEXIS CHANYL

FOR MERCY
LESSONS I WOULD HAVE TAUGHT MY DAUGHTER
ALEXIS CHANYL

Seed Planter Press

Published by Seed Planter Press, Santa Ana, California

Copyright ©2020 Alexis Chanyl
All rights reserved.

No part of this publication may be reproduced, stored in a retrieval system, or transmitted in any form or by any means, electronic, mechanical, photocopying, recording, scanning, or otherwise, except as permitted under Section 107 or 108 of the 1976 United States Copyright Act, without the prior written permission of the Publisher. Requests to the Publisher for permission should be addressed to Permissions Department, SeedPlanterPress@gmail.com.

Limit of Liability/Disclaimer of Warranty: While the publisher and author have used their best efforts in preparing this book, they make no representations or warranties with respect to the accuracy or completeness of the contents of this book and specifically disclaim any implied warranties of merchantability or fitness for a particular purpose. No warranty may be created or extended by sales representatives or written sales materials. The advice and strategies contained herein may not be suitable for your situation. You should consult with a professional where appropriate. Neither the publisher nor author shall be liable for any loss of profit or any other commercial damages, including but not limited to special, incidental, consequential, or other damages.

Copyeditor: Lynette Smith, www.AllMyBest.com
Proofreader: Clarisa Marcee, www.AvenueCMedia.com
Cover design and interior layout: Yvonne Parks, www.PearCreative.ca

Library of Congress Control Number: 2019915675

ISBN: 978-1-7341266-0-0 (Paperback)
ISBN: 978-1-7341266-1-7 (Kindle)
ISBN: 978-1-7341266-2-4 (ePub)

DEDICATION

For my son, who I love so much.

And for my daughter—it has not been in vain.
Thank you.

All my love,
Mom.

CONTENTS

INTRODUCTION

Three is a magical number in fairy tales; characters, trials, and wishes present themselves in trios. It is the first number of sides that can make a geometric shape, and it is the number that represents cycles of completion. Three is the number of creativity. It is the number of resurrection.

Three is also how old my daughter would have been at the time of this publication. I miscarried at three months pregnant, not long after having three cancerous spots removed from my cervix.

This book is inspired by my miscarriage, but it is not *about* my miscarriage. It is not a book about grief or loss, but rather it is a book about what there is to give and gain despite experiencing loss. A vast majority of us will lose someone or something of vital importance in our lifetimes. Loss does not define us, but instead provides us with an opportunity to redefine ourselves.

This is not a self-help book. I don't have the blueprint for a perfect life or a foolproof plan for anything at all. This is a book to remind girls everywhere that they are seen, they are important, they are smart, and they are beautiful. It is a book for anyone who is open to both validating and challenging the things they think and feel. It is for those who are receptive to their own transformation.

Above all, it is a love letter to my daughter, Mercy. It is an informal invitation to the dream world of my soul where I meet her.

If you find something in this world that helps you, you are welcome to take it. And if you don't, I am so thankful that you visited anyway.

MY LOVE FOR YOU KNOWS NO BOUNDS

This is my love letter to you. It is the lessons I have collected, lessons I share with you in spirit. The first lesson is the most important lesson and this is it: You are unconditionally loved. Nothing you could do in this world would push you beyond the limits of my love. For you, there are no limits. In your time of need, I will come to you—wherever you are. In your time of hurt, I will comfort you—with all of me. In your time of gladness, I will rejoice with and for you. If you are ever lost, I will bring you home. I will remind you of your sanctuary. I will be your place of refuge. My love for you knows no bounds—rest in this.

THE ONLY PERSON YOU SHOULD EVER TRY TO BE IS THE BEST, MOST EVOLVED VERSION OF YOURSELF

In a world of constant comparisons, know this: You, and you alone, are responsible for being you. Your job is to uncover the greatest version of yourself, and that has nothing to do with what anyone else is doing. You have been entrusted with gifts that have been hand-selected just for you. Your purpose cannot be completed by anyone other than you; no one on this earth can do the things you do just like you. Your work is to uncover what your thing is. There is enough work to be done in each of us without concerning ourselves with comparing our growth to the growth of the next person. Focus on your own evolution and flourish.

YOU ARE ALLOWED TO TAKE UP SPACE

As girls, we are socialized to be small. From the time we are old enough to play, we are generally encouraged to engage in activities that keep us quiet and stationary. In grade school, the boys can be found on the playground playing tag or any game that involves a ball, while we are taught that games like patty cake and imaginary play like house or school are better suited activities for us. Even more involved games like hopscotch or jump rope take up less space and are quieter than those typically played by the boys.

You may be conditioned to fade into the background and give boys the right to "just be boys," but you are equally allowed to take up space. You have the equal right to run far and fast, to be loud, to be free to be yourself, and not shrink just because society conditions you to do so. You don't have to own inferiority just because you're a girl, nor do you have to limit the things you want to do or try just because they are traditionally reserved for boys.

This stretches far beyond the schoolyard. You are not restricted to what society categorizes as "girl" things; gender stereotypes don't create well-rounded people. You are allowed to like whatever you like and pursue whatever you want to pursue. There is no glass ceiling under which you must stay, and there is no box into which you must fit. You are worthy of your individuality, and you deserve to occupy whatever space you wish to occupy.

LESSON 4

WALK WITH YOUR HEAD UP

When you go out into the world, walk with your head up. Don't look down at the ground or get lost in your phone—look the world in the face.

Be aware. Look people in the eyes, take note of who they are, and observe their behavior. You never know when you will need to recall the face of a stranger.

Have a presence about yourself. Boldly communicate your intentions with your body language. How you physically carry yourself affects how you feel and expresses the level of confidence you convey to the universe and the people in it.

Life is happening all around you. Don't let having your head down cause you to miss it.

REPRESENT THE GOD YOU WANT PEOPLE TO KNOW

When I moved from Northern California to Southern California, I started doing something I never did before: going to concerts. I love music, but sometimes being around that many people messes with my social anxiety. Stepping out of my comfort zone, I went to four concerts in a short time. All of the concerts were at the same place; and before every show, a crowd of people gathered across the street from the venue. Armed with picket signs and matching t-shirts, they yelled at concert-goers to repent or burn in hell. Obviously, they thought this was an effective way to reach people, but I really wonder how many lives they brought to Jesus by terrifying people as they went off to see their favorite performer. I wonder if they really believed God would approve of their conversion tactics.

Those people, and people like them who show up at various public events, remind me I never want to use that kind of approach in hopes of bringing people to God. The God I serve isn't mad at me, distant, boisterous, or waiting for just the right moment to send me to hell. My God is loving, patient, and merciful. When I lose my way, He fiercely seeks me out—not to chastise me, but to welcome me back into His grace with open arms.

If we believe God lives inside each of us, that means we get to use our lives as a vessel for His purpose. What if people only ever saw glimpses of God through you? What God would they know?

Would they know Him as a faithful father, or would they know Him as a condemning stranger? When they see you, would they even see Him at all?

Someone once said our lives may be the only Bible some people ever read; some people will only ever know Christ through their interactions with us. When you go out into the world, do your best to be a reflection of the God you want people to know. There is no way we can convince people the Lord is good and loving, if we ourselves are not.

God is who He is without any need for our opinion or approval. He is all powerful, all knowing, and all present, yet He never forces us to choose Him. He wants us to come freely by our own will. Fear can never genuinely bring people to Christ; they must come by way of love. We cannot scare people into following God, but we can love them so deeply that they become eager to get to know the source of that love.

LESSON 6

MANNERS MATTER

The more time I spend out in the world amongst strangers, the more I notice it feels like manners are dying out.

Not only do good manners reflect your own personal character, but they are also a tool to have a more positive day. Having good manners can even be the determining factor as to whether or not you get something you want.

If you walk in front of someone, say "Excuse me." If you go in front of another car while driving, put your hand up to say "Thank you for letting me pass." If you go out to eat, remember to incorporate "please" into your requests. Consider the difference in how you feel and are inclined to react when a person bumps into you at the store and says nothing, in comparison to the person who acknowledges the action by saying "Excuse me." Which person are you more likely to have a positive interaction with? Which person do you want to be? Being well-mannered shouldn't be a thing of the past— it's needed now more than ever.

LESSON 7

THE MOST IMPORTANT THING ABOUT YOU IS NOT HOW YOU LOOK

Ads powered by the beauty industry flood our everyday lives. By the year 2024, this industry will be valued at more than $850 billion. If you think you can block out the messages of the ads you see, know that only 8 percent of the thousands of ads you see on a daily basis are processed by your conscious mind. In fact, research shows that you need to see an ad an average of seven times before you even notice it.

An ad that's considered good by the corporations who fund it will always present unrealistic, unattainable images so consumers will continue spending their money on products and services in hopes of achieving displayed standards. The more we consumers relate how we look to how valuable we are, the more money is made by industries based on physical appearance. When greed is the name of a company's game, the worse we feel about ourselves, the better.

With all of the ads, billboards, articles, and products that target us so we will buy things so we can look "better," I want you to know that you are so much more than what you look like. You have so much more to offer than what is visible. If you could wrap your head around all of the things you are capable of being and doing, you would be astounded. You are genius. You are unique. You are wonderful. You are necessary. You are powerful. You are divine. And no product will ever exist on the market that can overpower the greatness that already exists inside of you.

LESSON 8

CALL PEOPLE BY THEIR NAME

For most of my life, I associated hearing my first name with either an overly formal greeting or with being in trouble. It wasn't until I got a job where we were encouraged to greet everyone by name that I learned the true value in doing so.

Salutations in which a person's first name (and/or last name when necessary or appropriate) is used not only show the effort you've made to remember their name, but also show you are paying attention to them personally. Using people's names instead of generalized group terms like "guys," "everyone," "y'all," etc. (or no name at all) is a subtle reminder to them that they are noticed in a world that is often just too busy to do so.

JUST COMMIT TO TEN MINUTES

When motivation is hard to find, use the "ten-minute trick" to get you started. Commit to giving ten undistracted minutes to whatever it is you're having a hard time doing.

If you want to exercise but can't even imagine making it through a whole workout, just tell yourself you're going to go to the gym (or wherever you work out) for ten minutes. If after ten minutes you want to leave, you can. If there's work you need to do but you'd rather do absolutely anything else, dedicate ten minutes just for the task at hand (no multitasking allowed). If your living space is a huge mess but cleaning it up feels like it would take ten years instead of ten minutes, just put in the ten minutes.

The likelihood is that after ten minutes, you'll find that you're willing to put in more than just those few minutes. It isn't uncommon for those ten minutes to turn into twenty or thirty minutes, an hour, or even enough time to complete the task entirely. Setting aside small blocks of time to be productive, when done often enough, creates the habit of working consistently as well as leaves room for breaks when they're needed. Even if you decide to quit after ten minutes, *some* time put in is better than no time at all.

SEIZE YOUR YOUTH

Growing up, I couldn't wait to get older. It was as if a magical land of freedom existed just beyond my teenage years. Fast forwarding, I realize that that magical land does indeed exist, but it comes with its own set of rules. Sure, I can stay out all night, but I'm still responsible for making it to class or work on time. Sure, I'm free to blow my money on anything I choose, but somehow that loses its luster when adult bills start to pile up. Sure, I can eat fast food for every single meal, but that soon catches up to my waistline. Sure, I'm free to do all of the things my parents never let me do as a kid—but not without real, grownup consequences.

The other thing no one ever tells you about getting older is that pretty much everything is either different or harder as you age. Socializing gets harder; the people in your life all have their own lives and schedules that make it difficult to coordinate a good time to get together. Going back to school as you get older is a totally different experience; as an adult, you generally have more responsibilities that, in turn, affect your ability to focus and your need to use your time effectively. Maintaining your health gets harder because your body has its own agenda and doesn't work how it did when you were younger. Just because you have limitations when you're young doesn't mean there are none when you get older.

Regardless of how old you are, today is the youngest you will ever be. Seize that youth and take advantage of the energy you have now. Growing older is a blessing many never get the opportunity to experience, but being young is equally a blessing. Don't take your youth for granted by being in a rush to grow up. A special kind of freedom exists in being young, and it's something you'll never get back.

YOU CAN'T EXPECT OVERFLOW FROM EMPTY CUPS

I love everyday metaphors. They are nature's way of reminding me that there are lessons everywhere; they remind me that life is always conspiring to put me in a position to grow. As humans, we tend to complicate things, but the things that exist and operate without any thought have the power to guide us when we need it.

One of my most called-upon metaphors is the metaphor of the cup. The cup represents the human vessel (you), and the level of the contents in the cup represents how full you are in terms of your happiness, love, security, and all other emotions and experiences. The more you know about the cup, the more insight you have about yourself and about others. Here is what you should remember:

1. *A full cup is your responsibility.* It's possible for outside circumstances or other people to add to your cup, but you can't rely on others to fill you up.

2. *Filling your own cup isn't selfish, it's necessary.* Take care of yourself. Do things that make you feel happy and full.

3. *Empty cups don't overflow.* Unless you're full, you'll have no way to spill over into others. It's difficult to be to others what you aren't to yourself. If you don't love yourself, it's hard to properly love others. If you don't feel happy with yourself, you will have a hard time being happy with others. Similarly, if you notice that someone else is having a hard time spilling over into you, it may be that their own cup isn't full.

4. *If you have a lid on your cup, nothing can come in and nothing can go out.* Be receptive to fullness; don't block your blessings by being closed off to them. Take the lid off of your cup to receive and to pour unto others.

5. *Fill your cup often—the contents evaporate.* Filling your cup, even to the glorious point of overflow, isn't a one-time deal. Just as water slowly evaporates, what's inside of you can slowly dry up without replenishment. Continue to refuel your soul.

The analogy of the cup always prompts me to ask myself two questions: *Am I expecting the right things from myself and others based on the fullness of our cups?* And *What can I do today to fill my own cup and the cups of the people around me?* The quality of your life reflects the contents of your cup. May your cup always overflow.

STILETTOS OFF THE BOARDWALK, PLEASE

Not everything I want to share with you is deep, poetic, or thought-provoking. Some things are just to save you some embarrassment. This is one of those things.

Unless you are some kind of mythical acrobat, it's probably best not to wear stilettos on a boardwalk or on any kind of wooden surface with ridges or knots. Maybe this is common sense to a lot of people, but I was not one of those people. At least not until I wore a pair of heels to a beachfront restaurant with a boardwalk and found myself literally stuck in the wood. I took a step, my heel got wedged in a gap between wooden boards, and my whole foot came out of my shoe. Of course, once wasn't enough. This same situation played out a total of three times, consecutively. Each time, I had to be helped back into my shoe but not before my barefooted self had to first yank my shoe from the wooden planks.

"Doing it for the fashion" sometimes has its consequences. I'm just trying to save your pride—and your ankles.

NUMBERS DON'T DEFINE YOU

Numbers rule the world around us. We are taught to aspire to things that can be measured and counted so other people can easily assign us a value. If we can't count it, we don't know how to rank it. And if we don't know how to rank it, simplemindedness takes over and leaves us confused as to how much attention or respect we should give it.

Who you are cannot be quantified. You are not a number, you are a divine being. What you are is greater than the amount of what you have.

The number you see when you step on the scale doesn't determine your worth.

Your GPA doesn't determine your worth.

The amount of followers, views, likes, or comments you get doesn't determine your worth.

The amount of money you have doesn't determine your worth.

Not only do numbers not tell the whole story, but anything you can count is also subject to dramatic, rapid change. And then what? Does your value instantly change just because the numbers in your life have? Your character cannot be boxed in by things you can count, and you will always miss out on quality if all you ever concern yourself with is quantity.

MAKE YOUR BED

If you want to start your day off on a good note, make your bed. It sounds so simple, but taking those extra three minutes in the morning to do this easy chore will help you feel composed and prepared for the rest of your day. Making your bed also starts you off with a bit of momentum that can begin your list of accomplishments for the day. At the very least, it gives you the ability to say, "If I accomplish nothing else today, at least I made my bed."

You'll feel put together and prepared in the morning, and comfortable and at ease when it's time for bed at night. If making your bed isn't already part of your normal routine, give it a try and see how it affects your mood.

GIVE CREDIT WHERE CREDIT IS DUE

The quest for originality is at an all-time high; no one wants to be known as the person who copies everything she sees. The thing about originality is that in its true essence, it is incredibly rare. Subconscious social influence is impossible to escape.

Apart from the influence you experience without realization, there is also the more obvious influence that happens when you see something you like. Whether you like material items, lifestyles, or behaviors, if the originator inspires you, one of the highest things you can do is give them credit for their inspiration.

People are so afraid that acknowledging another person or source will make them look less favorable; so instead they just pretend everything they do comes from their own mind and their own mind alone. Inspiration is cyclical and continuous; if people truly gave credit where credit is due, they would see how connected we all are and how we really are just one body inspiring each other.

If someone does something that motivates, encourages, or energizes you, say it. You never know what that kind of selfless recognition can do for another person.

LESSON 16

ANYONE WHO DOESN'T LIKE YOU, ISN'T YOUR CONCERN

You are not going to like everyone, and not everyone is going to like you; it's natural. Trying to get everyone to like you would not only be exhausting, but it would be impossible.

Be kind, be cordial, and be equitable, but don't give too much thought as to who likes you. Instead, ask yourself if *you* like you. *You* are the person you spend the most time with; are you the kind of person you'd choose to be around? Are you the kind of friend you'd want to have? Do you treat others well? Do you feel that who you are is in alignment with who you're meant to be? Are you being your true, authentic self?

If the answer is yes, great. If the answer is no, get to know yourself better. Embrace who you are, forgive yourself for past mistakes, know that you are good, and commit to studying yourself. Focus on self-evaluation, not self-criticism. The first will help you understand why you do certain things; the second will dig you deeper into the hole of self-hatred.

Have patience with yourself while you evolve. The process is challenging, but it's worth the effort. Whether or not you like yourself is far more important than whether or not the next person likes you.

LESSON 17

BE MINDFUL OF WHAT YOU SAY ABOUT THINGS YOU'VE NEVER EXPERIENCED

I had my son, Cartier, when I was 19. Being my parents' oldest child and the oldest of all of my cousins, I was used to being around kids, and I was good at caring for them. Even with having taken care of all of the kids in my family, it took my becoming a parent to realize that pretty much everything I thought about parenting was off.

Now it makes me laugh a little inside when I hear people who aren't parents go off on self-righteous tangents about how they are going to be when *they're* parents, what *their* life is going to look like, and how simple *they* make parenting seem. It makes me laugh because hypothetical parenthood is nothing like actual parenting. When you aren't a parent, you can't comprehend how the things you haven't experienced will affect you. Ask a person without kids how long it would take to get out of the house with a brand new baby, and then ask a new parent how long it actually takes. Compare non-parent to parent answers about how many outfit changes you should pack for an overnight trip with a three-month-old baby, or what it's like trying to teach your children things you've never learned. Ask parents and non-parents what it's like trying to raise their kids through things they themselves have not yet healed from.

There is no way to know what kind of parent you'll be until you actually are one; speculative opinion changes once you start experiencing things for yourself. The same principle goes for all other aspects of life. Be careful when saying your piece about mental health issues, abuse, trauma, or any other experience you've never lived through. It's natural to imagine what you'd be like in certain circumstances, but it's foolish to assume that everything will be just as you've imagined. Being a know-it-all about the things you don't actually know is the easiest way to separate yourself from people you could learn from.

WEAR YOUR FAVORITE OUTFIT TO THE GROCERY STORE

In my attempts to be overly practical, I have often left my favorite clothes unworn. While saving them for the "perfect" time is a tempting reality I often give in to, a little voice asks, *What if you never get the chance?* All too many dresses, shirts, and whatever else have gone out of style or gotten too small while hanging in my closet with the price tags still attached, all in the name of waiting for the "right" time.

My advice? Wear the outfit. Wear it to the grocery store if you have to. Are you overdressed? So what? Do you feel good? Good. When you look good, you feel good; and when you feel good, you do good. Don't concern yourself with whether or not you're being extravagant or with what other people might think of you. Concern yourself with the idea that you might unknowingly sabotage the you who is trying to accomplish something great because you feel the part.

It's not about the outfit; it's about how you feel in the outfit. The outfit is just a tool to boost your confidence and remind you what you're made of.

TAKE A LOOK BEHIND THE SCENES

Years ago, the production company for a reality TV show held a contest for a leading role in a movie from my least favorite genre—horror. My imagination is vividly overactive, so everything about scary movies freaks me out. This series let viewers into the behind-the-scenes world of how scary movies are made. Seeing a horror movie without the visual effects, CGI, and creepy music basically took away everything about it that made it scary. Seeing it this way reminded me that the things we see aren't always what they seem to be.

When it comes to media, in fact, things are rarely what they seem to be. Many of the things we see are scripted and calculated. Even the things that appear most organic are carefully planned to seem that way. If you get the opportunity to see how things are really made, take it. Not only will it give you a peek into reality, but it can also give you a newfound respect for the process of creating content.

Just as scary movies are not actually all that scary, real life is not as perfect or easy as it seems on camera, especially in regards to social media. Remember that not everything you see is real, and without seeing behind the scenes, you may be fearing, praising, or envying things that don't really exist.

YOU DON'T HAVE TO BE PERFECT TO BE WORTHY

My aunt used to have this sweatshirt that she wore all the time. This gray sweatshirt had holes all over it and a ripped neckline. This was not a trendy, distressed sweatshirt—this was a 23-year-old crewneck that had been washed 400 times and looked like it had been attacked by moths. Our family would always make fun of her for choosing this sweatshirt over all of the other clothes she had, but she never cared. It was her favorite and she loved it.

We all have something like this in our lives. Whether it's our favorite thing to wear or place to go, or even our favorite person, their imperfections don't keep us from choosing them. The worthiness of our favorites isn't dictated by how perfect they are.

So, why is it, then, that so many of us believe we have to be perfect before we are worthy? Why are we so hard on ourselves, always thinking that if we do just a little bit more, then we will be deserving of love or appreciation or whatever other sentiments we mentally reserve for when we are perfect?

My aunt would have had no problem buying a new sweatshirt, but it was the comfort of her old one that kept her going back to it. Eventually, it got so worn that people thought it was vintage and expensive. It was almost as if the more ripped it got, the better it seemed.

Not a single thing in this world is perfect, but innumerable things are worthwhile. If you can see the value in your imperfect favorite clothes, visit your favorite city without giving a second thought to the things about it that aren't so great, or love and care for another naturally flawed person, you can recognize that you too are worthy of being loved, respected, admired, and valued without having to be perfect.

TAKE IT IN STRIDE

When life gets hard or overwhelming, remember to take it in stride. There is a lot of pressure to think big picture or long term; and while yes, that is important, sometimes you can only muster the strength for one moment at a time.

While working jobs I didn't like, I focused on growing out of those jobs and taking in one chunk at a time. If I could work my scheduled days, then I'd have a day off. Some days I couldn't emotionally handle the thought of how long it might be until I could escape, but I could push through and work X amount of days, knowing that a day off was coming. I've heard marathon runners describe their process similarly. Telling yourself that you're going to run in five-mile chunks is more doable than telling yourself that you're going to run twenty-six miles at once.

Take it in stride. In life, you may work a job you severely dislike— take it in stride. You may get sick or hurt—take it in stride. You may have to make uncomfortable changes—take it in stride. You may have to mourn the loss of someone living or dead—take it in stride. Whatever it is, take it in stride.

The pressure of tomorrow will always be there. But what is the point in agonizing over what tomorrow could possibly bring, if just making it through today seems too unbearable? Take in what you can and relieve yourself. One day at a time, one step at a time.

LESSON 22

SLEEP IS IMPORTANT

At some point, someone in the Western world decided that sleep is for the weak. Our culture has long encouraged us to sleep less so we can work more. The problem with this philosophy is that sleep is one of our primary needs, making it the foundation on which all other functions are built. Our functionality is directly correlated with our quality of rest.

Now I'm not talking about just sleeping your life away, nor am I talking about temporarily losing a few hours of sleep here and there. I'm talking about confusing healthy and necessary sleep with the damaging idea that sleep is a threat to your productivity. Our society pushes the objective of reserving sleep for when we're dead, prompts us to brag about how little sleep we get, encourages us to pump ourselves with caffeine and prescription drugs to keep us awake, and then acts perplexed when a growing number of young people are dying from complications linked to said drugs.

Unless you're sleeping an abnormal amount of hours on a regular basis, sleep shouldn't be the first thing you think of giving up in hopes of adding more time to your day. If standard productivity seems like it just doesn't get the job done, it might serve you well to see if you are confusing being busy with being productive. Internal and external distractions can trick you into thinking you have less time than you actually do. You don't need less sleep, you need more focus. A couple of extra hours of sleep is a far better investment in your future than hours spent caught up in whatever the distraction of the day is. Get your rest—your body and your brain will thank you.

ANGER IS JUST THE TIP OF THE ICEBERG

The "tip of the iceberg" is a standing expression symbolizing that what is seen is actually only a very small part of the whole. Anger is a tip-of-the-iceberg type of emotion; when a person is angry, the anger stems from the triggering of other emotions. It is important to remember, when dealing with both yourself and others, to take a minute to dig deeper and consider what is truly at the root of the anger. Ask *Why is this making me/him/her/them mad?* Consider surrounding events, as well as what you know about your/their past experiences. By doing so, you can take on the problem that actually *is* the problem and not just the tip of the iceberg. Only when you begin addressing the real issue can understanding, healing, and transformation occur.

Expressions of anger range from person to person, but listed below are emotions/feelings that are often disguised as anger:

Embarrassed

Traumatized

Lonely

Frightened

Annoyed

Regretful

Stressed

Helpless

Nervous

Attacked

Anxious

Exhausted

Guilty

Insecure

Offended

Envious

Rejected

Distrustful

Overwhelmed

Disrespected

Disgusted

Uncomfortable

Disappointed

Sad

Worried

Pressured

Powerless

Obligated

Ignored

Inadequate

Vulnerable

Incompetent

YOUR BED IS NOT A STUDY SPACE

Having a comfortable bed is an unmatched blessing, but don't study or work from there if you want to keep your productivity levels high. It's way too easy for short study sessions to be dragged into long ones because the comfort is distracting. It's way too easy to doze off, no matter how much you convince yourself that you won't. Study or work somewhere that forces you, in the very least, to sit upright.

LESSON 25

DITCH THE CLICHÉS
ABOUT FINDING A MATE

We've all heard them... the corny yet oddly appealing clichés about how a significant other will somehow be the missing piece in our lives.

I'm not downplaying the fact that the right partner will or should indeed be a positive addition to your life. But overused phrases like *He completes me*, or *She's my better half* insinuate that one person is incomplete without the other.

You have no need to look for a better half—you are not half. And if you are half—if that much of you is missing—you ought to be out looking for *it* instead of looking for a mate. You are an entire being, all on your own. If you're going to be with another person, that person too should be a complete being. What can half a person do for you? What can half of a person even do for himself?

It is no one's responsibility to complete you, and it is not your responsibility to complete anyone else. Wholeness should not depend on the presence of another person, but should be an irrevocable reward earned once you have done the necessary work within yourself.

LESSON 26

JESUS WANTS TO TAKE YOU TO LEGOLAND

Flexibility is not one of my strong points—I am terrible with change. I'm bad with big changes, I'm bad with small changes, but I am the absolute worst with last-minute changes and changes that involve altering a course of action that I have already previously decided on and committed to.

One Sunday morning during church, Pastor Scott Martin told a story about his nine-year-old son, who shares my loathing of change. His son, like me, needs extra time to process that a change is coming. He needs to know what the change is and when it will happen.

Pastor Scott told the story of how one weekend morning, he and his wife decided to take their kids on a spur–of-the-moment adventure to the theme park, Legoland. His son, still unaware of the last-minute change of plans, had already mentally committed to lounging in his pajamas and playing video games for the day. So when Pastor Scott told his son to get dressed because they were going somewhere, he had a full blown meltdown. Relatable.

In the midst of his son's outburst, Pastor Scott shouted, "Buddy, buddy! We're going to Legoland!" Realizing that his plans for the day weren't ruined but instead were upgraded, his son let out a delightfully casual "Oh," went and got dressed, and spent the rest of the day having a great time at Legoland.

Pastor Scott reminded us that his son's initial response to a change of plans is so similar to how many of us react to God when He starts to do something unexpected. We kick and scream, seeing only the perceived likelihood that everything is going to be ruined because of change. What we don't see is that God is trying to take us to Legoland. He's trying to upgrade us, elevate us, and give us better than what we had or had even imagined.

We often hold on so tightly to things, we neglect to recognize that if we cling to one thing, we have no way to grab onto the greater thing God is trying to give us. The Creator of the universe is trying to take you to Legoland—will you let Him?

IT MATTERS IF YOU ARE AT THE TABLE

Fifty-one percent of the population in the United States is female, yet fields like politics, medicine, sports, entertainment, and science are still heavily male dominated—so much so that 90 percent of lawmakers in America are men. To say the need for a woman's voice in places of leadership is necessary would be an understatement.

The idea of women in positions of leadership is so threatening to male-dominated societies that those societies condition us to believe that a woman cannot be both a good woman and a good leader simultaneously. Neutral qualities normally associated with leadership are often credited as positives for men but negatives for women.

A man's dominance is seen as power; but if a woman is dominant, she is seen as domineering. If a man is stoic, his stoicism is perceived as strength; but if a woman is stoic, she is perceived as being cold and isn't well received. In politics, a man's family makes him seem well-rounded and relatable, but a woman with a family is made to appear distracted and conflicted in her obligations and responsibilities. This kind of hypocrisy undermines the value of women's representation. Look closely and you will see that many of the decisions that affect women are being made by men whose experiences differ vastly from those of their female counterparts.

It is critical that women who wish to lead do so not only for the sake of representing the voices of other women, but also to show girls of the future that they too can be leaders. It is difficult to be what you have not seen; if girls don't see women in power, they are less likely to recognize it's an option for them.

Your ideas matter.
Your voice matters.
Who and what you represent matter.

The characteristics you possess as a woman are a positive you can use to your own benefit and for the benefit of those around you.

The future is dependent upon the difference you are capable of making.

LESSON 28

PUT MAYONNAISE ON IT

I'm not even sure how or why this works; I just know it does. If you burn yourself, slather the burn in mayonnaise as soon as possible. Use a ridiculous amount of mayo on it, and then leave the mayonnaise on the burn for at least fifteen minutes. It won't heal the burn, but it will either minimize or erase the pain.

SAVE YOUR COINS

One of my fondest memories of my dad is of the time he unexpectedly came home with an off-roading Jeep. First we asked why; then we asked how. To that second question, he responded, "I bought it with my change!" My dad is a master at saving whatever money is in his pocket at the end of the day. It is from him that I learned to save my coins.

If you don't use cash or you're more of a digital person, find an app that will round up to the nearest dollar whenever you use your debit or credit card and save the change for you. You aren't likely to miss a few cents here and there, but those few cents can really add up over time.

THE HAND YOU'RE DEALT ISN'T AS IMPORTANT AS HOW YOU PLAY IT

I wouldn't consider myself to be a typically competitive person. But once, while using the inflight entertainment on an airplane, I started playing solitaire as a way to distract myself from the turbulence. The system allowed me to see my high score as well as the high scores of other passengers who were also playing. After my first game, I noticed that a passenger who was sitting three seats away from me was beating my score by 15 points. So, for the next three-and-a-half hours straight, I played with the sole purpose of beating him (which I never did).

I might be dating myself, which in itself is funny to say because of my age, but I love solitaire. When computers first started becoming a more common household object, solitaire was one of the few programs that came with the computer. This quiet, card-sorting game teaches strategy, requires thoughtful attention, and ends when the game is won by successfully revealing all cards and returning them to the four foundation piles that are organized by suit. The initial hand of cards is dealt at random, and like with most games, some hands start off looking better than others. Some hands look so undesirable, in fact, it is not uncommon for players to see their hand and immediately start a new game just to get a better first hand. The thing is, regardless of how many times a player restarts a game in hopes of being dealt the ideal hand, almost all hands are theoretically winnable just as they are.

"Bad" hands, when played skillfully and attentively, can still be successfully won. On the flip side, even the perfect hand can result in a quick loss if the player rushes through the game, ignores winning cues, or makes careless moves. It is the player—not the hand—that determines the fate of the game.

So often in life, we focus on what we have (or don't have) with such intensity, we overlook the fact that *the power is in what we do with what we have.* Many who have been set up for success from birth and are well equipped with resources of every kind, still manage to squander it all away. Then there are those who are born into the most unideal circumstances who create lives that far exceed anyone's greatest expectations. I'd be lying if I said all of our hands come with equal opportunities—life is unjust that way. While there is no restart button that allows us to opt for a brand new hand, we are each capable of creating the best possible scenario with the hand we've been dealt.

In solitaire, you can't win without uncovering the aces that make up the base of the foundation piles. Finding an ace in the game gives a sense of hope for a win. In life, the hope is not in a single card or even in the whole deck—it's in you, and you can make a winning hand out of any hand.

LESSON 31

YOU HAVE THE POWER TO TEACH PEOPLE HOW TO TREAT YOU

People will only ever do to you that which you allow. If you let people treat you as if you aren't good enough, they will continue to treat you as if you aren't good enough. If you let people take advantage of you, they will continue to take advantage of you. If you let people treat you poorly, they will continue to treat you poorly. Whatever you allow is what will continue, so be very clear about your expectations up front. If you require that people treat you with respect, they will have no choice but to do so. There are ways to demand this that are quiet, powerful, and classy. Your demand doesn't have to be forceful or emotional; it can just be very matter of fact. Expecting dignity is non-negotiable.

Your relationship with yourself is directly related to the standard you have in relationships with others. Having a standard obligates people to treat you well if they want to be around you. If their character doesn't match your standard, then you free up space for people whose character does. Some people won't want to stay in your life because of your expectations. You have to be okay with that. You have to decide what kind of people you want around you. Quality people have quality character. The people you lose because they refuse to treat you with kindness are not really people you lose at all.

If you notice people in your life treating you in a way you shouldn't have to tolerate, calmly call them out about it. It's possible they don't realize they're doing it. Address the situation early; the longer you wait, the more likely the undesired behavior will continue. Watch for their understanding and adjusted behavior over time. If their actions persist, take a step back and decide if they are really a good part of your life.

When I was pregnant with Cartier, one of my best friends at the time said some really terrible things about me and my unborn baby. I was hurt, but when she apologized, I realized she had a habit of behaving that way toward me. I told her I forgave her, but I didn't want to maintain a cyclically negative relationship with her anymore. And that was the end of our friendship. She never disrespected me or my son again because I removed all opportunity to do so.

People aren't perfect. You might not agree on everything and you might occasionally argue, but one thing you should never argue about is how you expect to be treated. You are in control of what you tolerate, and what you tolerate is what will continue.

DON'T USE EMPTY THREATS

Don't use threats as a way to force people into agreeing with you or as a way to scare people into doing what you want. Control your emotions. Find a better way to communicate your wants and needs. Threats, manipulation, and coercion condition people to associate negativity or fear with you. Once they realize they don't want to feel those things anymore, they will eventually pull away from you.

Don't use this method with your friends, your significant other, your kids, or anyone else. It's better to make no threats at all and act genuinely than to make empty threats that unnecessarily fill people with fear, sadness, or defeat.

LESSON 33

THROW OLD MAKEUP IN THE TRASH

There is usually a small jar symbol on the packaging of makeup and other personal care items. Pay attention to these manufacturer guidelines if you want to avoid a potentially nasty infection. Generally, mascara has a shelf life of three months, powder makeup can last upwards of two years, liquid foundation is good for about 6–12 months, and lip products need to be thrown out after about a year.

LESSON 34

CARRY A WATER BOTTLE WITH YOU

Hydration is important. If you're having a hard time drinking enough water, carry a reusable water bottle with you. Having the bottle in plain sight will remind you to drink more, and having it within arm's reach will make it easier to do so.

LESSON 35

THINK BEFORE YOU SPEAK

Whoever coined the phrase *Sticks and stones may break my bones, but words can never hurt me* seems to have never experienced the true potential of the things people say. Words have the power to build people up or to tear them down. What we say can affect how other people see themselves and how they act. Words may have never broken any bones, but they sure have broken a lot of hearts.

Think about what you say before you say it. Be slow to speak when you're angry. Harsh words, once said, can only be forgiven, not forgotten. Anger fades, but sometimes you may say things you can't take back. It's better to say nothing than to say something you'll regret. Not all of your words will be sweet, but make the effort to keep them from being bitter in the event that you should need to eat them.

Use your words to encourage the people you meet. Verbally express the positive things you notice and appreciate about the people in your life without assuming that they already know. Make it a point to emphasize the good you see in others—a kind word goes a long way.

IT DOESN'T HAVE TO BE GRAND TO BE GREAT

It's easy to get caught up in the idea that, in order to be effective in the lives of others (and yourself), you have to do something grand. In reality, it's the small things that make a big difference.

If you really want to do something great, look for the little, forgotten things. Cook someone a meal. Listen attentively. Be more understanding. Wash someone's car or remember someone's birthday. Take a walk with someone. Check in on someone you care about.

It's easy to overlook the abundance of low-cost ways you can love on others because you mistake the price of something with its value. Do the small things—that's where big impact is found.

CREATE A CAR FUND

If you're planning to drive or have a car, know that eventually, random things are going to go wrong with your car and, when they do, it's probably going to be expensive. Give yourself a little wiggle room by setting aside a few dollars here and there specifically for your car, and put the money in a place where you won't be tempted to spend it on something else.

New brakes, tires, timing belts, filters, and lights, among other parts, will inconvenience you less if you plan for them ahead of time.

LESSON 38

YOU CAN'T TALK YOUR WAY THROUGH A TOXIC RELATIONSHIP

A toxic relationship is one in which one or both of the people engage in behavior that is emotionally, mentally, and/or physically damaging to the other. This type of relationship isn't discriminatory—it can happen with friends, siblings, parents, significant others, co-workers, whomever. With any relationship, positive self-talk is a powerful tool that can help you navigate through conflict and internally work your way through problems before they escalate.

Unless you are the toxic person, you cannot use self-talk to turn a toxic relationship around. You will justify the actions of the other person, you will empathize, you will pity. And then you will stay. Over and over again. In a never-ending cycle.

When people you love are toxic, you will hope they will eventually become who you believe they are capable of being, but toxic people must heal themselves, before they are capable of having any type of healthy relationship with someone else. Even if they were seemingly willing to change for you, it would be disingenuous at worst and short-lived at best. People change only if they believe a change is necessary.

Don't ignore the toxicity. Someone's mother once said, "The things you ignore will be the reasons you leave." You may be so committed to the idea of what something should be that you'll turn a blind eye to who they really are. Toxic relationships cannot be fixed with a conversation, and you are worth so much more than what toxicity brings.

LESSON 39

DEFINE YOUR OWN STANDARD OF SUCCESS

One of the most important things you can do for yourself is to decide what success looks like to you. Define your own standard and disregard what anyone else is doing or what their opinion of your standard is. If you get too caught up in listening to what others think success looks like, you will model yourself after them and end up chasing their standard instead of your own. The danger in doing so is that if you succeed by someone else's standard, you still won't feel successful. Your success is tied to what fulfills you personally.

Just as you should live according to your own standard, so should everyone else. Don't use your standard to judge other people's success. And don't think that just because something isn't what you want for your life means that it isn't someone else's ideal life. Different people can be equally successful, even if their lives look nothing alike. Live and let live.

When you slow down and look at your life, how will you know when you've succeeded? Will your measure be that of your own happiness? Or will it be by how much other people agree with your version of success? You don't have to do what everyone else is doing. You don't have to want what everyone else wants. You don't have to let the world make you all the same.

LESSON 40

DO IT NOW

I am Queen Procrastinator. Not only do I have the habit of putting things off until the last minute, but I have even managed to justify it by convincing myself that I "work better under pressure."

In fourth grade, I waited to do a report on Native Americans until the night before it was due. In high school, I waited to do an entire summer's worth of book reports until three days before the start of school and ended up staying awake for more than 50 hours straight, just to finish. I have enough procrastination stories to put anyone to shame, but believe me when I say I am not bragging about my ability to get things done at the last minute. Some work turned out fine. Other work? Not so much. If there is one thing I know for sure, it's that procrastination has always cost me. It's cost me peace of mind, as I've been known to spend more time worrying about getting something done than actually getting it done. It's cost me money via late fees for all the bills I would "just pay later." It's likely cost me opportunities I don't even know about; if I could turn in slightly above-average work at the closing second of a deadline, imagine what I could have done had I properly utilized all of the allotted time.

In the deepest sense, procrastination can cost a sense of contentment. Life is short, and things may be left unsaid or undone because you think you have time. If you've ever had the misfortune of experiencing the deep regret you feel when you planned to do or say something that you find yourself no longer able to do or say, you know exactly what I mean.

Make a commitment to yourself that when it is within your control, you won't put things off until later just for the sake of doing so. Give up procrastination and do it now.

SOMETHING'S GOT TO GIVE

I read an article once about an incredibly famous wizarding author, J. K. Rowling, with the focus of the article being how she managed to write such successful books while being a low-income, single mother of young children. Rowling, now a billionaire, supposedly gave up housework in order to free up time to write. While I don't believe she just stopped any and all cleaning while conjuring up the wonderful world of Hogwarts, it is a deeply valuable reminder that prioritization is key.

There is a saying, "You can do anything, but not everything." It has become customary, and socially assumed, that we play multiple roles simultaneously. An amazing amount of pressure is exerted on us to be all things, do all things, and to be and do them well—all at the same time. As women, we can find ourselves striving to be students, employees, bosses, chefs, breadwinners, housecleaners, caregivers, chauffeurs, organizers, planners, problem-solvers, advice-givers, lovers, friends, tutors, and goal-achievers, or any combination of these and more. Whether we are doing these things for ourselves or for a family, the truth is that it's all too much. It's too much to be all things, all the time. There is so much focus on the things we're doing. But what about the focus on the things we're not doing? What are we allowing ourselves to give less attention to so we can give more of ourselves to the things that actually matter?

Maybe our collective addiction to mindless phone scrolling can take a backseat so we can be more present in the lives of the people we care about. Maybe we will have to learn that, before we can play therapist for all of our friends, we have to first work out some of the lingering kinks in our own lives. Maybe we will have to cut down from ten extracurricular activities so we can put our energy into the one activity we truly love. Maybe we will have to reevaluate our spending habits so we can spend less time working at jobs we hate just to support unnecessary spending habits. Maybe, like J. K. Rowling, we will have to concern ourselves a little less with immaculate baseboards and dust-free shelves so we can carry out the things that are saturated with our purpose.

Whatever great thing you are going to do will require that you temporarily *not* do something else. Something is going to have to give, and that is okay.

LESSON 42

MISTAKES ARE INEVITABLE

To avoid making a mistake would mean being a perfect person. While true perfection doesn't exist, the trap of perfectionism does. The perfectionist's mind is the trap that so often paralyzes forward motion. It is easy for good work to be left unstarted or incomplete because thoughts of inadequacy cloud what we are capable of doing. Perfectionism isn't birthed because we want to be better than someone else; it is birthed because we are afraid making a mistake would reveal that we are incompetent and thus unworthy.

One of the keys to life is to know, while we strive to completely avoid making mistakes, doing so is inevitable. We get so caught up in focusing on never messing up that we overlook the necessary skill hidden in mistake-making. Living a mistake-free life isn't an accomplishment—knowing how to work through mistakes is.

A mistake is an opportunity to grow, not a definition of character or a foreshadowing of your fate. Be less afraid of mistakes themselves and more aware of the consequences of making mistakes without learning from them.

IT ISN'T ALL YOUR FAULT

I never realized how much I subconsciously picked up from my parents until I went to the store for the first time after moving into my own apartment. Looking at the contents of my shopping cart felt so familiar—the items, including the brand and the sizes of the packaging, were all exactly what my mom normally bought. On future trips when I had to buy a cheaper brand of soap or a different kind of toothpaste, I felt a little off, like I was somehow being untrue to what I knew.

This feeling went beyond what I put into my shopping cart. When I didn't know who to be, my automatic response came from the part of my brain that had been silently studying my parents for my whole life. How I handled conflict, how I showed love, and how I created solutions for a variety of problems were all things I picked up from my parents. I didn't just internalize which brand of laundry detergent to buy; I internalized habits, tendencies, and mindsets.

My parents never sat me down and explicitly said "This is the kind of tomato sauce you should get"; they just did it, and I followed suit. When you mimic what you've seen, it's normal—it's a way to be included and a way to belong. The trouble comes when you pick up things that are harmful to yourself or others. And these things are learned just as easily as which grocery items to buy.

You may have learned things in your life that have been the source of unintentional disservice. You likely don't even realize you've adopted negative ways of being from the people around you—that is, until you are exposed to new ways of being that make you want to change or until you have caused enough hurt and have no choice but to change. Regardless of what you do to change or the reasons behind why you stay the same, the point is that you didn't just become the way you are all on your own. You got it from somewhere. The parts of you that are hard to make sense of, or the parts that create cyclical patterns resulting in unwanted outcomes, often stem from things that aren't your fault at all. Adopting the patterns of the people around you is natural and, in some cases, it's survivalism.

While what you learned may not be your fault, it is still your responsibility to correct it; none of us are exempt from self-correction. Your parents, grandparents, caregivers, neighbors, or whoever else influenced your lifestyle each have their own things they were working through, both then and now. They too were loading their shopping carts with familiar items. Your job is not to fault them, but to understand them, forgive them, and then heal yourself.

I love instant ramen noodles; I grew up eating them and would probably still eat them if the amount of salt didn't give me a sickening sodium overdose. It wasn't until I got older that I realized eating preserved wax noodles twice a day probably isn't on the list of the best things I can do for myself. The same can be said for my excessive worrying and my lack of flexibility.

Maybe it's time to start looking at which of your habits don't serve you well. Maybe it's time to take a few things out of your cart—like the ramen. Or the negative self-talk. Or your financial frivolousness or poor communication skills or abusive tendencies. Not everything you've learned to put into your cart needs to make it to check-out. Not everything you've learned needs to be a permanent part of how you live.

LESSON 44

DON'T TALK YOURSELF OUT OF DOING GOOD

Often, when we have a thought to do something good for someone else, it is almost too easy to reason ourselves out of actually doing it. We think, *What if it doesn't matter? What if he doesn't care if I do this for him? She probably doesn't need it anyway. It'll take too long. It'll cost too much. Someone else will do it if I don't. I'll just do it next time.* Our brain ping-pongs between questions and possible scenarios until we talk ourselves out of acting on our initial thought.

Don't reason out of doing good. Don't let that little voice of self-doubt creep in and convince you that what you're moved to do isn't needed. Genuine acts of compassion are never done in vain. Imagine if everyone acted on positive impulses instead of holding back, having been won over by the thought that it doesn't matter anyway. Be the person who acts. The world needs as much kindness as it can get.

LESSON 45

FAMILIARIZE YOURSELF WITH THE NEWEST TRENDS AGAINST WOMEN

In a perfect world, this conversation would never be needed. In a perfect world, we women could go out alone at night, trust strangers, and be less cautious about the people we hang around with or date. But this isn't a perfect world. Even if we should be able to do the things mentioned above, the reality is that women are still targeted and victimized. Kidnapping is real. Human trafficking is real. Crimes against women are real.

Familiarize yourself with the tactics being used to lure women from safety to danger. Aggressors are creative, and their methods change frequently. Pay attention to the things that are going on in the world. We are being lured in by the crying of fake babies, by drugs disguised as candy, by spiked drinks, and by seemingly innocent strangers. We are caught off guard by other women who claim to need help while a male assaulter waits nearby, by fake threats, and by enemies posing as friends. Attackers disguise themselves so well that we often don't realize their true identity until it's too late.

Stay safe by being aware. Stay in public, well-lit places; and when possible, stay in a group or with another person you trust. Be prepared: Have what you need (like your keys) in hand and don't stand around looking through your purse or bag. Lock your car when you get in and while you're getting gas, even in the daytime. Learn how to escape from zip-ties or other materials that can be used to bind your hands or feet. If you're getting a ride from a taxi service, make sure you're getting in the right car. Don't leave your drink unattended, and don't take substances from people you don't know. If you ever feel someone is following you, call the police and either drive or walk to a police station or another public place—do not lead the person who's following you to your home. Be smarter than your potential attacker by recognizing the sign of trouble before it happens. Above all, keep your eyes open and trust your gut instinct. It's better to be overly cautious and safe than to silence your inner voice and end up hurt or dead.

LESSON 46

BREAK BIG TASKS INTO SMALLER PROJECTS

Whenever you find yourself stuck in a rut that makes everything seem overwhelming, create momentum with mini accomplishments.

Start with something simple. Your living space plays a big role in how you feel; if your personal space is cluttered, your mind is likely to be as well. Walk around where you live and make a note of everything that needs to be done. Start with the things that will take you less than ten minutes to complete. Put away that pile of clean laundry. Vacuum. Take the trash out. Move on to working on things that will take you less than an hour, and try to fit in one a day for a week. Then look for the things you have specifically been putting off. Is something broken that needs to be fixed? Does something need to be organized? Does anything need to be physically removed or added into your space? Commit to tackling at least one of these tasks at a pace that works for you, meaning you're going to actually follow through and not just tell yourself that you will.

Let this strategy spill over into any other area of your life you might be struggling with. Wherever you are stuck, start by doing a little. A little more than you did yesterday, or a little more than you think you can today. By focusing on small accomplishments, you will build up your confidence by reminding yourself how capable you are. You're also likely to find yourself motivated by your own work. If you feel you can't do a lot, you can create movement in your life by just doing a little.

LEND ONLY WHAT
YOU'D BE WILLING TO GIVE

One of the greatest feelings is to be able to stand in the gap for people you care about and be the connecting factor between what they have and what they need. If you find yourself in a position where you have agreed to help out by lending money, the best thing you can do for yourself is to consider the money you lend as being gone the minute you lend it. And I mean gone. As in gone forever. Never to be returned or repaid. In case you haven't already noticed, people aren't always as reliable as you hope they'll be. They don't always do what they say they're going to do, and they don't always return what they say they're going to return. I've found I'd rather convince myself that any money I lend is a gift and be pleasantly surprised if I do get it back, than to be thrown off because I never got the money back and I had higher expectations of the person.

I'm not saying you shouldn't inquire about your money or hold people accountable for paying you back—you absolutely should. What I am saying is that it's wise to start by setting boundaries regarding whether you're in a financial position to lend out money in the first place, how much you're able to lend, and when you expect to be repaid.

You are under no obligation to lend money; there's nothing wrong with saying that you can't or won't lend someone money. You are also under no obligation to lend the full amount that's requested if it's more than you can afford to give away. You are allowed to decide when you expect your money to be returned to you. Even when internally operating from the mindset that you won't be getting your money back, you don't have to tell borrowers you're not expecting to see the money again. Setting a timeline to be repaid will let them know you are holding them accountable. Setting these boundaries before you ever give out a single dollar will communicate to borrowers that you have expectations about what will happen after the money moves from your pocket to theirs.

Living from the perspective that money on loan is money long gone will keep your relationships from dissipating over money, and it will keep you from getting into your own financial predicaments while trying to help someone else.

LESSON 48

CONSIDER WHAT YOU'D MISS

Today's culture encourages us to contemplate what's missing from our lives and how it would be different if we had those things. Rarely are we reminded to look at what we'd miss if what we have now were to suddenly disappear. The truth we all know but don't truly feel until it's too late is that life can change quickly; and when it does, we are usually unprepared in some way.

Take advantage of what you have right now. Take advantage of where you are right now. Look at your life and consider what things you'd miss if they were to unexpectedly go away. Whether these things are big or small, act on appreciating, caring for, and making the most of them.

Two of my most prized possessions are my photos and my random free-writes, both of which I keep in my phone. I've learned, on multiple occasions, that electronics are fragile and it only takes a second to lose all of the information stored on them. If you're like me and you keep valuable things on your phone, would you feel secure knowing that you've backed up your pictures, notes, calendar, contacts, or whatever else if your phone was destroyed today? What if your schedule or daily routine permanently changed? Would you feel good with how you're spending the time you have? Or would you feel that you may be wasting time, energy, or resources, not realizing how quickly life can (and does) change? What if tomorrow someone you love were to leave this earth? Would you feel confident that you'd made the effort to let them know how important they are to you?

You are human with human limits—you can only do so much. It might not be practical or even possible to act on every single thing you'd miss if your life were to change, but you can start with focusing on just one thing a day. Send a text to someone you haven't spoken to in a while. Spend five minutes imagining what it would be like if you suddenly lost one of your senses, and do something to honor the fact that you have that sense today. Spend a little more time appreciating the good that is in your life right now.

The acquisition of more, new, or different things is what we are pushed to aspire to, but the maintenance of what we already have is a dying virtue. Don't wait until it's too late to develop a deep sense of gratitude for what you have.

DON'T LET SOCIETY TELL YOU HOW TO BE HAPPY

Living in such a digital age, we are conditioned to believe that happiness should look a certain way. We are bombarded with images of people swimming amongst a hundred stingrays in the Bahamas, and couples spooning in beds that overlook the skyline of world-renowned cities. We are flooded with stories of people who pack a seventy-two-hour workday into a single twenty-four-hour frame and have too many accomplishments to count. We are overloaded with video clips of smiling faces powered by material items, status, and power. Don't get me wrong; when experiences are executed genuinely, they are beautiful and worthwhile. But happiness doesn't look just one way.

Do you know where I've experienced supreme happiness? Reading a book under the covers of my bed in the middle of a summer day while the air conditioning is on full blast. I've been supremely happy watching the sunset or sunrise. I've been supremely happy with little and I've been supremely happy with much. I have been supremely happy at places and during times when society would have preferred to rob me of my bliss by convincing me that it wasn't enough. The thing about happiness is that it's subjective; what makes a person happy varies from one individual to the next. You will be as happy as you decide to be. Satisfaction is a choice, not an outcome.

Why be so invested in what society says happiness should look like, anyway? Most members of society are unhappy and unfulfilled, especially the ones who so loudly, publicly claim the opposite.

Pay attention to what makes you intensely happy and run with it. Maybe you'll feel extraordinarily happy eating a sandwich. Maybe you'll find unshakeable joy while climbing a mountain. Maybe you'll find the purest delight while laughing with your friends or in the presence of your family. Maybe you'll feel the happiest doing the most extravagant thing you can think of, or maybe you'll feel ultimate contentment when sitting down to do absolutely nothing. Wherever you find your joy, remember: You are the master of your own happiness.

LESSON 50

IF PEOPLE ARE TRYING TO BE FAITHFUL, LET THEM

I've observed this weird phenomenon with women that goes something like this: Imagine a woman doesn't pay any particular attention to a certain man. Time goes by and that man gets a girlfriend or a wife. Suddenly, now that the man is taken, the woman has an abundance of interest in him and attempts to pursue him. Or, similarly, the woman knowingly pursues a man who is already in a relationship. The happier the man appears to be, the more she is motivated to pursue him.

The woman has convinced herself that the happiness the man has with his current significant other is the happiness he can (and should) have with her instead. The most twisted part about this scenario is that things can never work out the way the woman imagines. She can never have what another woman has with a certain man because she is not that woman. A relationship isn't one-sided; it's a two-part equation. If you change one part of the equation, the outcome will always be different.

This doesn't apply only to relationships. It also holds true in the cases of people who may be trying to give up smoking, drinking, certain foods, bad habits, or parts of a lifestyle that do not positively serve them. If people are working to be committed to something positive, the last thing they need is a selfishly motivated person coming along to throw them off their game.

If people are trying to be faithful, let them. Be a supporter, even if you have to do it silently or from afar. Be an encourager instead of the devil on their shoulder saying that giving into temptation won't hurt. Giving into temptation does hurt; don't be the reason for another person's hurt.

LESSON 51

UNCOVER YOUR "SO THAT"

Social psychologists believe all humans have two common social desires: to be liked and to be genuine. In a competitive society, our need to be liked often trumps our need to be authentic, eventually creating a sense of confusion within us. How is it we can do everything to be well liked by our peers yet still feel empty or inadequate inside?

I once heard a radio talk show host say you should give good thought as to what your "so that" goals are. A "so that" goal is one you dissect until only the root of the goal is left. By examining the root of your desire, you are forced to ask yourself, *Who or what am I actually doing this for?*

Think about a goal you have, or something you feel you want, need, or must do. Now, add the words "so that" after the goal and fill in the blanks to complete the statement. Continue doing this until you've reached the root or foundation of your goal. Once you're there, consider if the motivation behind your goal is in alignment with how you want to live your life.

Here is an example: I have struggled with body image since I was eight years old. For as long as I can remember, I have always felt I should weigh less than I do. If I apply the "so that" technique to my need, it might look something like this:

- "I need to exercise every day."
- (So that…?)
- "… So that I can lose weight."
- (So that…?)
- "… So that I can look like [insert name of current Instagram model I've been comparing myself to]."
- (So that…?)
- "… So that people will like me better."

This "need" of mine is rooted in my desire for people to like me, with the basis of their acceptance being my physical appearance. The actual goal of exercising every day isn't inherently bad, but the root of it doesn't match the frequency on which I want to operate my life.

The approval of society is fluid, fleeting, and potentially dangerous. Author Cornelius Lindsey warned that if we live for the approval of man, we will die from man's criticism. If at my core I believe I should live for the approval of my God, but my actions center around seeking the approval of man, it is no surprise I would never feel at peace with myself. Trying to hold two contradictory beliefs simultaneously presents a no-win situation.

The same goal with a different foundation not only matches my desire for authenticity over superficiality but is healthier overall. The healthier "so that" version of the same goal might look a little something like this:

- 'I need to exercise every day."
- (So that...?)
- "So that I can be healthy."
- (So that...?)
- "So that I can (hopefully) live longer and have a better quality of life."
- (So that...?)
- "So that I can be around as long as possible for my family."

This need is rooted in having a long, healthy life that will benefit me and the people I love. This root better matches the things I want to be rooted in.

If I am desperate for people to like me and I believe the only way for me to achieve that is to be thinner, missing a workout could be a cause for a meltdown, clouding my thinking with negativity and hurry. If I see exercise as a means to being around longer for my family, I will see immediacy as being far less important than consistency. I will have planted my worth in who I am and who I aspire to be, rather than who I think others expect me to be.

By rooting ourselves in authenticity over approval, we give ourselves the gifts of grace and patience. In so doing, we give ourselves permission to be imperfect, and in our imperfections is where true beauty lies. I challenge you to dissect your own goals and to be honest about why you do the things you do.

LESSON 52

KEEP A CAR KIT

Always keep a stash of things in your car that you might need. Below is a list of items that typically come in handy and might even save your day. Most of them will fit in a cosmetic bag or pencil box that can go in your center console. The bigger things that won't fit there can go under your seats, in your glove compartment, or in your trunk.

$5 to $10 in cash

Floss

Candy

Gum/mints

Travel toothbrush

Mini lint roller

Deodorant

Lotion

Bandages

Phone charger

Tampon/pad

Pen/pencil

Lip balm/lip gloss

Tissues/napkins

Hairbrush

Hand sanitizer

Perfume/body spray

Stain-removing wipes

Nail file

Hair ties/hair clip

Chewable medicine for an upset stomach

Aspirin/ibuprofen

$1 in quarters

Umbrella

Mini sewing kit

Small flashlight

List of emergency phone numbers

GIVE YOURSELF SOMETHING TO LOOK FORWARD TO

Every Wednesday I go out for coffee with my best friend, who also happens to be my sister. Hanging out with her is my mid-week adventure that pushes me through the first half of the week and recharges me for the second half. This time with my sister gives me something to anticipate every week.

Our dad has always told us that we have to give ourselves something to look forward to. Doing so will get you through hard days and keep your life from feeling mundane. You will always have bills to pay and responsibilities to carry out. Pick something you love and plan for it, even if it's something small. Break up your week by setting aside one morning, afternoon, or evening to slow down and do something you don't get to do all the time. Reserve one day a month as a day you do something outside of your normal routine. Grab a smoothie, plan a trip, or take a nap. Put whatever you choose into your schedule just like you schedule work or sleep or household chores, so in moments of struggle you will have something to push you to keep striving. It's important to have long-term goals, but it's equally important to have small objectives you can reach for monthly, weekly, or even daily.

LESSON 54

BEFORE YOU FLASH YOUR LIGHTS, GO AROUND

I'm not a great driver, but I am a good driver. I use my blinkers and follow the speed limit, much to the annoyance of the people who want to drive a hundred miles per hour on the freeway. One of my biggest pet peeves as a driver is when people honk or flash their lights from behind when there are open lanes all around me. Do they really have to go eighty-seven in a forty-five zone in *this* lane? Is riding my tail really that necessary when they could just merge over? Is all that road rage really worth it?

What is the point of wasting precious energy on getting mad or upset when something is within your power to change? Look for ways to "go around" in life. Solutions to your problems are often readily available, but you may spend too much time complaining about outside circumstances to see them. You can't expect other people to move for you; you're going to have to take initiative. Before you get aggravated because it seems like something is inhibiting you from reaching a goal, seek out other ways to get there. Why flash your lights when you can just go around?

IF YOU HAVE A PRIVILEGE, USE IT FOR THE BENEFIT OF OTHERS

The word *privilege* has an elementary association with things we did or did not get to do as kids. Our behavior was often the deciding factor as to whether we lost or gained certain benefits. As we get older, we realize there is so much more to the word *privilege* than just not being able to watch TV or go out with friends or whatever other temporary restriction or permission may have been presented. Privilege has less to do with consequence or reward and everything to do with unearned advantage.

These advantages, often granted because of membership in certain groups, are present and working at all times. Privilege is recognized most often by the people excluded from its benefits. Below is a brief description of a few of the most prevalent privileges in our society today, along with a few examples of what they look like in everyday life.

- *Gender privilege* pertains to the general favoritism of men. It can be seen in the gender-pay gap in which women make roughly seventy-nine cents for every dollar a man makes for equal work. Men generally worry less about sexual harassment and/or rape than women do. Having children does not typically affect a man's career or how he is viewed in the workplace. Many career fields are completely male dominated and, unlike women's appearance, a man's appearance is not a main determinant of worthiness or capability.

- *Religious privilege* favors Christians, as Christianity is the main religious group in the United States. Christians generally can freely worship without fear of persecution. When making a legal oath, swearing on a Bible is the norm. Christmas music is played during the holiday season, and Christian holidays are typically days off from work. Entire schools are dedicated to the Christian faith, and it is likely that teachers will share the same faith as their students.

- *Socio-economic privilege* favors individuals of higher social class or societal standing. These people typically don't worry about being hungry or homeless. They assume their basic needs will be met. They are able to purchase things out of desire and not just out of necessity. They have freedom to focus on pleasure and the enhancement of their lives by way of goals, growth, and expectations for the future.

- *White privilege* applies to all white people regardless of other advantages or disadvantages. History taught in school is written mostly by whites. Whites tend to be favored in the judicial system and have a generally more positive relationship with the police. They are often favored by school authorities, and schools are still systematically segregated through geographical affluence. Children's books feature mainly white characters, and even characters of different races usually have white features.

- *Heterosexual privilege* favors heterosexual individuals. It is assumed that everyone is straight. Heterosexuals can show affection in public without fear of ridicule or hate crimes. They can have joint custody of children and can be granted immediate access to hospitalized loved ones.

- *Cisgender privilege* favors individuals who identify with the gender that matches the biology they were born with. Cisgender individuals can use public bathrooms, store changing rooms, gym locker rooms, and other public facilities without fear of harassment. Their gender identity is accepted without question or outside opinion.

Privilege is so prevalent that it often goes hand in hand with judgment and discriminatory acts. There are people who are harmed on a daily basis solely because they do not have the same privilege that others do. If you benefit from a certain privilege, here is something to remember: It doesn't matter if you don't agree with another person's lifestyle or beliefs when that person is harmed for not being a part of a group that experiences the same privileges you do. It doesn't matter if you don't think people should have different sexual orientations or identify with a different gender or be of a different race or social class than you. It matters that people without that same privilege are undeservingly punished for being who they are. You are entitled to your opinion, but you are not entitled to unearned security, safety, and comfort while others suffer because they're different from you.

If you are fortunate enough to be part of a group that experiences the benefit of privilege, the best thing you can do is to recognize your privilege by stepping outside of yourself and imagining a life without it. Because privilege is unearned, you have no control over whether or not you have it. You don't have the right to brag about it, nor does anyone else have the right to put you down because of it. It matters not what privilege you have, but what you do with it. With this realization comes both responsibility and opportunity. When used correctly, privilege can provide a pathway toward societal progress for a multitude of people.

Powerful are those who use their advantages to be allies for those who don't have the same advantages. As an ally, you probably will not have had the same experiences as the people you're standing with, and that's okay. It's better to know that you can only ever understand externally than to reach for connections that aren't there. As a heterosexual woman, I can only understand the discrimination of lesbian women on a surface level because I myself have never experienced it. To try to match their struggle would be to minimize it. You don't have to live a certain lifestyle to know discrimination against those who do is wrong.

The voices of the privileged are heard when others are ignored. Be tolerant. Be inclusive. Speak up where you see injustices. I remember watching a video recorded in a courtroom where a black man stood up to speak against what was being said. Police officers from every angle drew their guns, and when they did, a group of white men and women stood around the black man, facing the police with their arms up in protection for him. These individuals recognized the power of their racial privilege in the presence of authority. They served as a moving example of people who acted, without hesitation, to stand with a man who could benefit from what they had.

Do you have a privilege you can use for the gain of others? Is there something you can do to make the world around you a little more equitable? Are you willing to see differences as the place you can step in and use your advantage for the advancement of someone else? It's not living the same life or always seeing eye to eye that's transformative—it's walking hand in hand even if you don't. Banding together when you're the same is powerful, but banding together when you're not is radically impactful.

LESSON 56

DEVELOP A PERSONAL MANTRA

Come up with an easy-to-remember phrase you can say to yourself when you need encouragement or reminding, and incorporate this saying into your daily self-talk. Every morning, and all throughout the day, I ask myself, *Who is the me I want to be?* This mantra forces me to slow down and really think about whom I want to be and if I'm doing what needs to be done to be that person. My mantra takes me off autopilot, guides me toward practicing self-discipline, and reminds me to stay focused on what is most important to me.

Pick a phrase that most speaks to you. It can be a reflection of what you want for your life as a whole, or it can be specific to certain areas. The mantra itself won't be enough to keep you on track, but it will keep you present and intentional, and those two things have the power to change your life.

TAKE GOOD CARE OF YOURSELF; SOMEONE LOVES YOU SO MUCH

Some days, it might feel like it doesn't matter how you live or what you do. There might be days when you feel like you just don't care about yourself at all, or days when you're having so much fun that you don't even think about taking care of yourself. On those days and at all other times, it's important to remember life is not an isolated experience. It isn't something you go through alone, even on days when you feel most lonely. Someone, and probably several someones, deeply care for you.

What you do has the power to affect the people you love, so remember them when you make choices. This is not to say you should live your life for other people or never take chances or make changes; instead, it reminds you to keep the people you love in your mind in times of carelessness or indifference. Think about how what you do impacts them. Use the love of the people who care about you to motivate you to make good decisions for yourself.

Texting and driving is incredibly dangerous—this fact cannot be argued against. Yet those who continue to text and drive think all of the research and evidence about how it affects driving applies to everyone except them. They think they won't be the ones who crash. Anytime I have made the poor decision to pick up my phone while driving, I remember who I would hurt if I were to crash, even if I was the only one in the crash. The people I care about keep me from being careless on the road because I love them enough to want to keep them from the potentially negative consequences of my actions. Even if I think what I'm doing is harmless, I know I would never want to be the reason for the heartbreak of the people around me if I was wrong.

What you do matters. How you live matters. Think twice about your actions and remember that things affect not only you. Make good decisions and take care of yourself. For you and for them.

LESSON 58

OPINION ISN'T LAW

Just because someone thinks something doesn't make it true. And just because you think something doesn't make it true either. Opinion is just that—one's own thoughts about something.

If someone thinks something bad about you, so what? It's one opinion. One perspective. And there are hundreds of those. Don't take on the views of others without doing your own research, and stop internalizing things people say or think about you based on their own judgment. Even good opinions can sway you the wrong way if they aren't coming from the right source.

Know that not everyone's opinions are based on reason and that opinions change all the time. Your opinion isn't the law, and neither is anyone else's.

PASSIVE AGGRESSIVENESS KILLS RELATIONSHIPS

It's been said that holding onto anger is like drinking poison and expecting other people to die. The same is true for being passive aggressive.

When people are passive aggressive, they mix their anger with their desire to be understood. Simply, they express a lack of communication skills. This breakdown in communication has the power to ruin relationships.

If you want to be effective (and mature), get really clear about what it is that you want to say, and then just say it. The person you're trying to reach is more likely to be confused, offended, or angered by your passive aggressive behavior than they are to change to meet your expectations. If you're passive aggressive, it's more likely that other people will either be oblivious to what you're doing or purposely ignore your behavior so you're forced to speak up, than it would be for them to take in what you're saying and respond in a productive way.

Passive aggressiveness only tells part of the story. Save your time and your energy by just being straight up.

YOU AREN'T THE MOST INTERESTING PERSON IN THE ROOM

It doesn't matter how many trips you've been on, how much money you have, who you know, or what you've accomplished, you are not the most interesting person in the room.

Even if you have traveled the world, have a wealth of knowledge in a plethora of fields, have friends in high places, and have had so many experiences that you lose count, every interaction you have with others shouldn't be just about you. Even in your most enlightened days, you will never know everything. It is not God's design that our own understanding be sufficient to get us through life. People need each other; and, by knowing this, you should recognize each person you meet has something to teach you.

Foster discussions that allow other people to share their passions and experiences with you. Don't just wait for a break in the conversation so you can switch the focus of the narrative to you—actually listen. Learn to engage, ask good questions, and make eye contact. Be open to what others have to offer, even if your experiences differ. Lessons aren't always explicitly revealed— sometimes what you learn through other people extends beyond what is said in a conversation.

Conversely, you are not the least interesting person in the room, either. You have things of value to contribute. Your experiences and thoughts are worth sharing and have the power to impact others. Don't be afraid to speak up, and don't confuse humility with passivity. You are above no one, and you are below no one. Everyone else has something to give, and so do you. Never dim your light or second-guess your gifts. Humble yourself, but always honor yourself.

LESSON 61

EVERYTHING IS AN EXPERIMENT

A few years ago, I decided I was going to try to learn how to be less hard on myself. I wanted to give myself more grace and let go of so much self-criticism. My sister and I started saying, "It's an experiment!" to everything we did—especially when we had no idea what we were doing. When people asked us why we were pursuing things that didn't make sense to them, we would just say, "It's an experiment!" When we started to doubt our own ideas, one of us would tell the other, "It's fine! It's an experiment!" We reminded ourselves and each other often that we were experimenting and were under no obligation to know what we were doing.

Truthfully, none of us really know what we're doing, anyway. We are all just trying to find our way, and that requires a lot of trial and error. Seeing your life as an experiment removes the pressure of expected perfection and replaces it with room for wonder, hope, growth, and excitement. No one expects an experiment to be perfect—it's a test to see whether or not something works. If it works, great! If it doesn't, you reformulate the experiment and try again. Think about it like those TV shows where a mad scientist is shown mixing the contents of random test tubes. Usually a few blow up in the scientist's face until something revolutionary is created. Life is the same. A few things might result in unwanted explosions, but ultimately finding out what doesn't work leads to the discovery of what does. Each experiment teaches you something about yourself. Each experiment is an experience, and experiences are how you grow.

To succeed in an experiment, you need only pay attention. Ask yourself often, *What did I learn from this? What can I learn from this?* Even a so-called "failure" is a step toward success. There are no losses.

In what areas of your life can you remove unnecessary pressure and begin using the experiment approach? What things have you been wanting to try but haven't yet tried because of the fear of unexpected outcomes? If you ever find yourself in a position where you start to wonder whether something you're doing is worth it or if it will work out, simply tell yourself that it's an experiment and continue on confidently in the direction of your goals.

Experimentation gives us an ongoing project to work on and something to always look forward to. No one has it all figured out, but we each do have the opportunity to see ourselves as a scientist in charge of discovering just the right mixtures for our own lives.

USE YOUR VOICE RESPONSIBLY

Like everyone else, you have been gifted with a voice, with the ability to influence others; and with that voice comes a responsibility in how you use it. Your voice and influence is amplified with the power of social media, as your beliefs are reflected in your posts, and what once may have been kept to yourself or within your immediate circle now becomes accessible to the world.

Not long ago, after the death of a world-renowned chef who took his own life, I was clicking through Instagram stories and, as with most celebrity suicides, encountered numerous posts wishing this man the peace he couldn't find here on Earth. I remember clicking the icon of a woman I was following to find a written rant about the stupidity of people who commit suicide. She went on to say how this man got what he deserved, how he was selfish, and how no one should give him any attention or remembrance, because of the way he died. This woman had a significant number of followers, many of whom are statistically likely to have been personally affected by suicide in some way. The insensitivity of her comments reminded me that many people use their public platforms to speak poorly about people they don't understand.

We have a right to our opinions, but opinions turn into a different kind of beast when they are rooted in ignorance. This woman had carelessly overlooked the blessing that neither she nor her loved ones had ever wrestled with the true darkness that precedes suicidal thoughts and actions. She mistakenly classified suicide survivors and victims as selfish, undeserving people instead of seeing them for who they truly are: People in need of love, people in need of hope, people in need of help. If we were able to speak to those who have lost their lives at their own hands, I am certain we would find that death wasn't nearly as appealing as was the desperation for their suffering to end.

Without realizing it, this woman used her gift of a voice to shame individuals who would have been better served by her silence than by her ignorance. Without realizing it, she quite possibly planted a dangerously negative thought into the mind of other people who may have been too weak-minded to form their own. This is how the cycle of ignorance is perpetuated; it is the blind leading the blind.

We are all influential to someone. Use your influence with caution. Post wisely, speak wisely, live wisely.

LESSON 63

THERE WILL ALWAYS BE SOMETHING TO BUY

Don't feel compelled to buy something every time you step into a store or see a promotion online. There will always be sales, there will always be new products, and there will always be something to buy.

If you have a problem with unnecessary spending, set guidelines for yourself. If you are an impulse buyer, tell yourself that you are going to wait a predetermined amount of days before you buy the thing you've been eyeing. This will give you time to decide if you really want or need it. If you have a problem with spending more than you can afford, set a financial prerequisite that you must meet before you can make any unneeded purchases, such as having to save three times the cost of an item before you allow yourself to buy it. If you have the habit of spending just to spend, set goals for your money and consider whether the things you're buying are getting you closer to those goals.

You don't always need to buy something. Ignore the pressure of consumerism, practice self-discipline, and save your money for things that serve a purpose beyond instant gratification.

BETTER TO UNDERPROMISE AND OVERDELIVER THAN TO OVERPROMISE AND UNDERDELIVER

Chill out with the people pleasing. You are one person. You can be only one place at a time. There is a limit to how much you can do in a given timeframe. Refrain from making commitments you can't keep in hopes of gaining people's favor. It might seem admirable to look like you can do everything, but it's honorable to actually follow through and do the things you say you will.

Stop saying yes to things you can't do. Don't book overlapping engagements in your schedule and promise to be at both at the same time or agree to deadlines you can't meet. Your best bet will always be to be honest about your abilities. If you can meet a request, kudos to you. If you can't, say you can't. If you're unsure, say that it's possible you will show up or do what's been asked of you. Give the other party the opportunity to handle whatever is needed in the event that you are unable to. It's better to underpromise and overdeliver than to overpromise and underdeliver. One leaves room for delight and surprise, the other leaves room for disappointment. Which one do you want to provide?

LESSON 65

JUST BECAUSE IT'S YOUR GIFT DOESN'T MEAN IT WON'T BE WORK

Somehow, our generation developed this idea that if we are gifted at something, it's going to always be easy; and if isn't easy, we're either off track or we're wrong about our gift. Don't fall victim to this mindset. No matter what you do, it's going to take effort. Athletes may be naturally skilled at their sport, but without practice and discipline, natural skill gets overshadowed by others who are willing to put in the work.

There are so many sayings and clichés about not forcing things and that "What will be, will be." While there is some truth in these, it is also true that if you just sit around waiting for what you think is meant to be, it'll probably never happen. Great things in life don't just happen—they are the product of divine order, mental manifestation, and hard work. If you confuse "work" with "force," you will be conditioned to give up when you're striving toward something that isn't happening right away. Many things that are truly worthwhile in life are going unclaimed because, the minute something isn't instantly rewarding or pleasurable, people drop it to find something that is.

A hedonist is a person who believes that pursuing personal pleasure is the point of life, and our society is filled with them. Living for the pursuit of pleasure keeps many from their destiny because destiny is rooted in action, and action can be uncomfortable, tiring, time-consuming, and hard. Putting in work can sometimes feel like the exact opposite of pleasure. But if you are unwilling to work, you are undeserving of the reward.

Your gift will still require work. You can be born with a unique, natural ability and still face times when you feel off track or tired to the point of wanting to give up. Even the things that are meant to be will demand that you do your part.

LESSON 66

SAVE YOURSELF

Life is full of sacrifices, particularly when you get older and you realize that other people count on you. Friends, family members, kids, and even strangers will need you, and you will find yourself making sacrifices for them. Do that. Make the sacrifices. Give wholly. Discover fully that life is so much bigger than just you, and that we all need each other if we are to thrive in this world.

One thing I sincerely advise, however, is to never give so much of yourself that you become bitter. If you find yourself in a position where you are giving, or have given, so much that you're becoming resentful or keeping track of everything you give, refocus your giving.

Giving out of guilt or obligation instead of giving out of desire and love is giving done in vain. What is the point in giving if you have to wear a mask that says, "I'm so happy to do this for you," only to cover a soul twisted in anger? What is the point in giving only to keep score? What is the point in giving if you've given so much that only a shell of yourself is left behind?

LESSON 67

LEARN TO BE OKAY WITH PEOPLE'S NOT KNOWING

The modern world is driven by the public display of private lives. The trend of excessive sharing is so popular that there is a silent obligation to use social media to constantly share what we're doing, who we're doing it with, and why we're doing it. This expectation causes us to miss out on the fullness of things in our lives because we are so focused on proving we have those things to people we know and to strangers, alike. It is not uncommon for people to spend more time viewing their lives through the lens of their phone or vlog camera than through their own eyes. *Sharing* an experience has taken over actually *having* the experience.

Not everything needs to be shared. The more we become accustomed to sharing our every move and thought, the more of a habit it becomes. The longer we have a habit, the harder it is to break. Many of us don't realize how much of our power we give away when we give people free access into our lives. By doing so, we unavoidably become swayed by the opinions and expectations of those people. We create images for ourselves, using our social media platforms to showcase things we think will validate those images. We start to question if people will think our lives aren't good or fun because we aren't showing it off. We think about what people want to see us post and, most concerning, we worry that people will forget about us if we don't post. We forget that life in its fullness still existed before everyone started sharing everything online.

The world is becoming increasingly obsessed with popularity and large-scale validation; it no longer matters if you're happy, as long as you can make it look like you are. For some people, avoiding a social-media centered life is no problem. For others, it can feel impossible to step away from that life. The goal is to find the healthiest space for you. That space can be found where your life is not ruled by what you see, hear, post, or don't post online. You don't owe insight or explanation to the world. Your life is *your* life, and it's crucial you keep some things just for you.

IF YOU HAVE TO FALL, FALL TOWARDS THE BUSHES

As a mom, I find one of the hardest things is knowing that pain in inevitable; at some point, your children are going to get hurt. As tempting as it is to try to keep my son in a bubble, ultra-protected by his mother's overcautious spirit, I recognize that the reality of doing so would actually be more harmful than helpful.

Bike riding is one of those activities where I wish I could just wrap Cartier up in a bubble suit with the biggest, most durable helmet ever known to mankind. I wish I could freeze time and make all of the cars immobile until he mastered looking both ways at all times and learned to steadily navigate without crashing.

One morning while taking on a new riding route with a steep downhill that was unfamiliar to Cartier, I heard my dad tell him, "If you have to fall, fall toward the bushes, not the street." Instead of my anxiety-ridden hope that my son wouldn't fall at all, his Grandpa advised him to take a calculated risk. He reminded him to think about what he was doing before and while he was doing it; and if he could sense himself falling, to fall where he would be less likely to be seriously hurt.

Falling is inevitable; failing is inevitable. While sometimes you cannot foresee failure, you can set yourself up to better take a hit. You can prepare yourself by thinking ahead, giving yourself some wiggle room, and being clear about what your goals are. If my son's goal was to conquer a giant hill on his bike, my dad wanted him to know that he could conquer the hill even if it meant he might get a little scraped up in the process.

There are many success stories of people who jumped, risking everything, with no backup plan. It isn't impossible to succeed greatly with that as your story, but I'd be willing to bet that most people will say, given the choice, they would choose having a safety net over not having one.

Are you planning to do something financially risky? Have some money saved. Are you planning to do something physically risky, like trying an extreme sport for the first time? Don't go alone. Are you planning to do something emotionally risky? Be secure in yourself and know you can handle what is to come. Great risk precedes great reward. Not every chance you take can be prepared for in advance. But when possible, if you have to fall, fall toward the bushes.

LESSON 69

BE SURE YOU AREN'T' SEEING WITH INSECURE EYES OR HEARING WITH INSECURE EARS

Everyone has insecurities. Even the most confident people have things they don't necessarily love about themselves. For the insecurities you haven't yet worked through, keep them under control by being aware of them. When you're insecure about something, it's easy to hear or see things through a distorted lens. Insecurities left unchecked turn innocent situations into big problems because your mind is already fixated on the belief that you come up short somewhere.

Having too much self-doubt can cause you to make yourself the center of things that aren't even about you, and that can cause you to take responsibility for things that aren't your fault. It also potentially robs other people of their right to feel how they feel because your insecurities make you think everything is about you. If you lack self-confidence, you might get mad at a group of people who laugh when you walk by because you assume they're laughing at you, even if they never actually saw you at all. Or, if you think you aren't good enough for your partner, you might internalize it every time he or she has a bad day. Even if how your partner is feeling isn't about you or taken out on you, you still blame yourself because you figure you must be the issue.

Not everything is about you. Not everyone is looking to prey on what you perceive as shortcomings. Don't let your insecurities be the reason something harmless escalates into something hurtful.

LESSON 70

DON'T BORROW AGAINST YOUR FUTURE SELF

The greatest temptation is instant gratification. As a culture, we want what we want, and we want it now. We are so set on having what we want, when we want it, we will make deals with ourselves, idealizing that the version of ourselves who exists in the future will have a better grasp on things and won't need certain resources as much as the version of ourselves that exists right now does. We spend money we don't have and count on future us to pay the bill. We plan on using tomorrow's energy to handle a task so we don't have to do it today. We ditch self-control and tell ourselves we'll make up for it tomorrow. We try to avoid discomfort by doing the fun thing now and counting on future us to do the work later.

Well guess what? The future version of each one of us has future plans. Future you doesn't want to exercise for five hours at one time to make up for the entire cake you ate today or pay the credit card bill for something you enjoyed six months ago. Believe it or not, future you is a lot less willing than you think to take on extra work because of what the current you wanted to do right now.

When you can avoid it, don't borrow against the future you because, whatever it is, your future self is going to need it too. Try to figure out how to make do with a little less now so you don't have to rob a version of yourself that doesn't even exist yet.

LESSON 71

IT'S ALL A LIE

For so long, I found myself heavily seeking what I've come to call the "triplets of deception." This trio does everything in their power to make you believe that as soon as you conquer them, you'll finally feel like you can take a deep breath and start to enjoy your life. These three are familiar to pretty much everyone, so I would like to reintroduce you to Security, Completion, and Control. Here is what I have ultimately found about them.

Security is an illusion, completion is a myth, and control is a fallacy. These three things don't actually exist; they are a modern day metaphoric mirage. Water in the desert is so appealing that we will use our last bit of strength to run to it, only to realize that each time we start running, the water looks just a little farther away. It looks just close enough to make us think we can reach it, so we keep trying. We do this over and over again until we realize we'll never reach it because we cannot possibly reach something that isn't actually there.

The truth is, we will never feel secure enough. There will always be something that we'll want to feel just a little more sure of. A sense of completion is a moving target. More than likely, before we've finalized one thing, we've already begun thinking about the next thing we plan on tackling. We are never actually done, we just find new things to work on. Even when we think we have control over a situation, we will always find elements that are completely out of our power. We can take the most calculated perceived route and still have things turn out in a way that we could never have foreseen.

Many people spend their lives in pursuit of these unattainable imaginings, only to be disappointed that it always feels like they're coming up short. They put off things they want to see or do because they convince themselves it'd be best to wait until they are just a little more secure or a little better established, or have a little better grasp on their lives. That time isn't coming; that time doesn't exist.

It's been said that life is a journey, not a destination. We're all headed somewhere, but none of us are headed to that fantasy land where everything lines up perfectly at all times. The faster you can make peace with that realization, the faster you can free yourself from a lifetime of chasing illusions.

MAKE A LIST OF ADVENTURES

One of the most valuable things I started doing in recent times has been making a list of adventures I want to have over the course of the year. I write my list on a big, heavy-duty poster board, and I keep a picture of the completed board in my phone so I can reference it at any time. I store the board in my closet and pull it out every day while I'm doing routine tasks like brushing my teeth or doing my makeup.

The adventures on my board range from trying the coffee at a new shop across the street from where I live to reading a certain amount of books to making sure I take my mom to lunch a certain number of times to visiting a country I've been dreaming of. Most of the adventures are things I've never done before, but I do include duplicate adventures from previous lists if they were worthwhile enough to make me want to do them again. It doesn't matter how big or small the experience is; if I want to do it, I write it down. Nothing is off limits.

Making this list keeps me intentional with how I spend my free time. Open time without a plan of action is easily wasted, but having a list of things you want to experience makes you more likely to go out and do it. Whether the adventure of your choice is to go across the world or to go across town, prioritize it. Whether you prefer spontaneous adventures or well-planned ones, keep adventure in the forefront of your mind. Don't just make a list; commit to making the things on your list an active part of your life. If lists aren't your thing, make a vision board with pictures of things you want to do. Whichever way works for you, create a visual representation of what you want your life to be made up of. Don't give a second thought to whether or not something seems likely or realistic. Every year, I purposely include adventures on my list that I have no idea how they will come to fruition, and many of them do. The repeated viewing and reading of your list plants your desires in your subconscious mind and will move you to look for ways to achieve them even without your conscious effort. You may find that things align because you have used your energy to call them into alignment.

At the end of the year, I take some time to review my list. I don't pressure myself to get every single thing done (my lists are always more than 100 adventures long), but I do mark off what I've done as I do it. The things I didn't cross off get sorted in one of two ways. Either I count it as being included on next year's board, or I recognize that I didn't actually care too much about having that experience after all. Either way, I win; either I have a head start on my next board or I've saved time and money by not doing something that didn't really matter to me anyway.

Let your whole life be an adventure, not just a collection of responsibilities that you're trying to make it through. By creating a personalized plan of how you want to spend your year, you will live on purpose, enjoying more of what you want and less of what life hands you by default.

LIFE IS A PUZZLE BOX WITHOUT THE LID

Imagine you are going to put together a puzzle. While you could use a few different strategies, everyone can pretty much agree that at some point you will need to look at the picture on the lid of the box. Depending on the intricacy, without this guide it would be impossible to put the puzzle together. You could begin with the pieces that make up the edges and try to build inward from there, but ultimately you would have no idea what kind of picture the pieces were supposed to come together to make, nor would you know which pieces belonged where.

Now consider that your life is the puzzle we're talking about, and each moment of your life makes up one piece to the puzzle. Even if you think you know what image you're working to piece together, you don't have the lid to the box. Even if you think you know where you're going, you don't have access to the whole picture. Some things will happen to you that won't be part of what you think the picture of your life should look like. So what's the use in worrying yourself to death about how everything will turn out, when you haven't got the box lid to your puzzle? What's the point in trying to force unfitting pieces together, when it is very possible that just because they don't fit in one spot doesn't mean they won't fit at all?

God holds the lid to your puzzle box; He knows how things will look in the end. He graciously gives you pieces, little by little, to keep you from being overwhelmed. Sometimes they fit right away and sometimes they don't. The pieces that don't seem to fit aren't trash, and they aren't misplaced from other puzzles—you just don't have all of your pieces yet.

Let go of the pressure to make everything fit right now. If a piece doesn't fit in one spot, it may very well fit in a completely unexpected part of your puzzle.

Put the pieces together as you can, trusting that when you are finished with your puzzle it will reveal a masterpiece of a story that is uniquely your own.

LESSON 74

THEY AREN'T LOOKING AT YOU LIKE YOU THINK THEY ARE

If you've ever worried that people were looking at you, watching you, and judging your every move, chances are they're not. The spotlight effect is a psychological experience that causes people to believe they are being noticed more than they are. Because we are each the center of our own lives, our brains automatically make the assumption that everyone else notices the things about us that we notice about ourselves. What we have a tendency to forget, though, is that others are also the center of their own lives and they all believe everyone else is noticing what they notice about themselves. So if I think you're noticing everything I do and you think I'm noticing everything you do, we're both wrapped up in ourselves and don't have much awareness for what the other person is actually doing. In fact, it takes something really big or making a direct call to attention before most people notice the thing you're hoping they don't. That's why a stain on your clothes isn't noticeable until you point it out, and why no one cares about the pimple on your chin until you mess with it and make it impossible not to see.

People notice less than we think they do, and they remember less than we think they do. If you do something embarrassing or have something you're self-conscious about, it isn't the big deal you think it is. Most of the time, the people who intentionally seek out and pick apart other peoples flaws are so deeply insecure themselves that they are just looking for a way to validate their own flaws. Worry less about what other people think. They either notice for a split second, don't notice at all, or notice only because what they're noticing matches what they hope no one notices about them.

LESSON 75

PUT YOUR PHONE DOWN

If you ever see me ranting about something from afar and you have to guess what it is, always guess "cell phones." I feel strongly about many things, but few as strongly as I do about how smartphones affect our relationships and quality of life. Maybe it's because I'm part of the last generation to remember what it was like to live daily life without the constant presence of a phone. Or maybe it's because I'm highly attuned to my surroundings and see more people lost in their phones than not. Either way, I can't help but notice the way technology in general has begun to reprogram us.

I'm not knocking all of the positive advancements that technology provides; I personally benefit from them every day, several times a day. What I am knocking is how disconnected we all have become, despite being more connected than we ever have been. We're happy to be able to video-call loved ones in other time zones, but we ignore the loved ones right next to us in exchange for just a little more time on our phones.

Cell phone activity is highly addictive; it's created to be. The more we use our phones, the more we feel we can't live without them. Routine moments of downtime, like riding an elevator, waiting in line, or sitting at a stoplight, are no longer filled with small talk or observing our surroundings; instead, those moments are used to scroll, post, or chat. Our phones are not just a tool, they've become a crutch. We've become awkward without them. We don't know what to do with our hands or where to look or what to think about. We worry that we won't look important or that we're missing out on something.

Do yourself a favor. Put your phone down. I know asking you to do it all the time isn't realistic, but make a habit of putting it down throughout the day. Put it down and put it away. Refrain from constantly needing to check it while you're in public and especially while you're in the presence of people you care about. Nothing is sadder to me than when I'm out and I see a child who is longing for the attention of a parent who's more concerned with his or her cell phone.

You don't have to search everything that comes to your mind right when you think of it. I promise you'll be okay if you don't immediately Google how tall Jesus was or how many seeds normally come in an apple. You don't have to answer every text, call, or mention as soon as it comes in. There was a time when people had to call you on your house phone if they wanted to talk to you (meaning you had to actually be at home in order to answer), and if you weren't there, they had to leave a voicemail on a machine that got checked periodically. And everyone managed. People still had successful relationships and businesses. The world went on, even without the immediate responses we've become conditioned to expect.

We're becoming accustomed to watching people live instead of living our own lives. You don't have to record every moment of your life. You can go outside and have a full experience, even if no one else knows about it. You're not weird for trading screen time for time spent being present and in touch. Too many people would be more satisfied with a scratch and sniff screen that lets them smell virtual flowers than they are with the fact that nature provides actual flowers for them to smell.

Our cell phones make us so artificial. We spend a large part of our lives seeking stimulation, validation, and gratification from a fake world that exists behind a screen. By regularly putting your phone down, you will be more aware, more productive, and more secure. You will free yourself up to be a source of attention and affection for your loved ones instead of leaving them to feel that they have to compete with your electronic devices. At the very least, putting your phone down will make you happier. A break from constant comparisons, overstimulation, unnaturally bent necks, and eye strain is just what you need to remind you that the real world is what's happening outside of your cell phone.

LESSON 76

DOUBLE-THINK YOUR NEGATIVE JUDGMENTS ABOUT OTHER PEOPLE

I once had a professor who asked the class about the general perception of a person whose phone rings loudly during a movie being shown at the theater. We agreed that our first reaction if someone else's phone goes off is that it's because they carelessly neglected to turn it off, because they are inconsiderate, or because they're a jerk. The professor then asked, "What if it were your phone?" The class responded that it would be because we accidentally forgot to silence it or that it was an emergency. It's funny how quick we are to have a valid "reason" for the unfavorable things we do, but judge other people's "excuses" for doing the same thing.

It's important to remember that everyone is going through something, and more than likely it's something the outside world knows nothing about. See yourself in others, relate to them, and practice empathy. Being empathetic doesn't mean you don't hold people accountable for their actions; it just means you seek to understand them instead of judging them.

It's easy to criticize and condemn people without knowing their full story, even when we know we wouldn't want someone to do that to us. Counteract this by giving grace; you never know when you will be the one who needs grace.

LESSON 77

MOTHERHOOD ISN'T THE MANDATE

Being a woman comes with assumed roles of all kinds. Many of those roles go unchallenged because it is normal for us to see the majority of women adhering to these societal expectations.

One of those assumed roles is motherhood. The Motherhood Mandate is the philosophy that the ultimate fulfillment as a woman is to become a mother. This ideology is both damaging and alienating, as it makes us believe that without children, we are incapable of reaching the fullness of what it is to be a woman.

You do not have to be a mother. Being a mom doesn't define you as a woman, and neither does *not* being a mom. It is more respectable for a woman to know that she doesn't want children, take positive preventative measures to avoid pregnancy, and not have children than to know she doesn't want kids and let society pressure her into having them anyway.

If you've decided you don't want to be a mom, people will try to convince you that you'll change your mind—and you might. But it's also okay to not change your mind. There is nothing wrong with you if you decide motherhood isn't for you.

There's plenty of talk about what it is to be a mom, the *whens* and *hows* of becoming a mom, and what to do if you're having trouble conceiving. There's plenty of talk about delaying motherhood and what is and is not ethical about pregnancy, but there isn't enough talk about all the things that make it okay to never want to be a mom, ever. This isn't about not being able to become a mom, it's about supporting the women who know for themselves that they don't want to be one.

Some women want to be the fun auntie to the kids of their friends and family. Some women are perfectly happy being mamas to the fur-babies of their choice. Some women don't want to have any kind of mothering role to anything or anyone at all, and that is okay. Whatever you choose, choose it for you. Motherhood doesn't guarantee fulfillment, and being childless isn't a sentence for an empty life.

LESSON 78

IT'S OKAY TO BE SAD

As women, our emotions are a weapon often used against us. Show too little and they say we're cold and disconnected, but show too much and they say we're unreasonable and unstable. This lose-lose mentality pushes us into the "I'm fine" response. There is a whole population of people whose world can be crashing down around (or within) them, and they'll still say they're fine—not because they really are, but because they don't want to seem incapable or weak. They don't want to publicly show too much emotion, out of fear of overreacting; and most of all, they don't want to seem like a burden to those around them. Every day, many women suppress how they feel, suffering silently, and covering it up with the ever so popular "I'm fine."

You don't have to be fine. It's okay to feel sad or down or confused. It's okay to be angry or discouraged or just a little bit off. It's okay to feel whatever it is you feel. If you're wrestling with a negative emotion, it's important to allow yourself to wrestle with it. Confront it. Seek to understand where it came from. Too often we women either accept our negative feelings, invalidate them, or ignore them. The acceptance of something negative without challenge can make us feel defeated and hopeless. We internalize the possibility of the negative being true, but we reject the possibility of something positive being true for us instead; we are quicker to internalize that we are worthless than we are to internalize that we are worthy. By invalidating our feelings, we tell ourselves that we aren't allowed to feel them because they aren't real or they aren't right. We minimize the truth behind what's going on inside of us, and by doing so we create further confusion and dismay. Telling yourself you aren't allowed to feel something doesn't make the feeling go away, it just makes you feel even worse for having ever felt it in the first place. Ignoring negative emotions can be equally as harmful. If you put a rug over broken glass, the glass will still be there for you to sweep up later. The way to conquer negative feelings isn't around them, it's through them. If you want bad feelings to go away, you have to address them at their core.

Acknowledge how you feel, and reach out for help when you need it. Admit when you feel low to people you feel comfortable confiding in, and don't assume that if they don't reach out first that it means they don't care. Don't be ashamed of how you feel, and don't hide it; you can't heal from what you hide. Don't say you're okay if you're not. Know everything will work out, but you don't always have to be "fine" in the process.

LESSON 79

BE A MAGICIAN

Good magicians always have something up their sleeve—at least figuratively. They always have a trick people aren't expecting and are prepared if something doesn't go according to plan. Good magicians don't stop or get stuck if something starts to go downhill, because they are good at thinking on their feet, and they always have a way to maneuver and recover should their trick go south.

Be like a magician. Create options for yourself. Be able to do what people don't expect, and keep something up your sleeve. This way, if and when situations arise, you won't have to rely on other people to save you. Being able to take care of yourself doesn't mean you don't need other people; it just means you won't be dependent on them.

Know how to manage your household in all aspects. Know how to physically defend yourself. Be well equipped with knowledge and creativity. Know how to take care of things in your life, or at least know where to go if you don't know how to do it yourself.

Be aware of your resources and opportunities, even if you have to create them for yourself. Set yourself up in such a way you know you can count on yourself to get the job done, regardless of who or what else you have in your life.

DON'T APOLOGIZE FOR WHAT YOU WANT

When you study how the mind works, you eventually get really good at recognizing patterns. In school, I could get around learning math lessons in their entirety because I could catch on to the pattern of how the problems unfolded. Without realizing it, I came to also do this with people; I could learn so much about them by just evaluating their patterns.

During one of my shifts as a waitress, a woman who was possibly subconsciously peer-pressured by her salad-ordering friends, ordered a salad and a side of fries. It wasn't what she ordered that was intriguing, but how she ordered. After ordering her salad, she said, "and I'll have a side of fries. I'm sorry."

Why was she sorry? Was she sorry to me or to herself? Did she believe she shouldn't *have* the fries? Didn't *deserve* the fries? Shouldn't *want* the fries? Was she concerned her ordering fries contradicted her ordering a salad? It wasn't just this woman; it was a multitude of women who ordered things and either began or ended their request with an apology. I can confidently say that I never personally served a man who was "sorry" for what he ordered.

It may sound silly, but the truth is that this pattern exists in other places besides restaurants. Why is it that many women apologize for ordering what they want? It's almost as if we say to the world, "I know I ordered motherhood, so I'm sorry for also ordering a career." Or "I know I ordered a marriage, so I'm sorry for still valuing and needing my independence." Or "I know I ordered gentleness, so I'm sorry for also ordering strength." Somewhere in our lives we women have been taught to believe that not only should we not order seemingly contradictory things, but we should be sorry for even wanting them in the first place.

If you have ever apologized for ordering fries with your salad, I challenge you to adjust your perspective. Instead of feeling like you should be sorry for what you ordered, I dare you to see yourself as brave. Many women always order only salad because they are secretly afraid of the scrutiny they believe will come to them if they do otherwise. Many women settle for only one thing when they were indeed created to be multifaceted.

Order the fries without apologizing. You deserve all you desire, even if you've been conditioned to believe the things you want don't go together.

LESSON 81

STOP TRYING TO GET AVERAGE THINKERS TO VALIDATE YOUR BIG DREAMS

A person who thinks on an average frequency cannot validate your big dreams; their minds aren't equipped for it. So if you're going to dream big, you had better get familiar with being misunderstood and slightly alienated.

When you think outside the box, it will be foreign to a lot of people. They will likely encourage you to stay small, like them. It isn't that they don't want you to accomplish your goals; it's that they either can't relate to your goals or have no idea how they would accomplish their own, so they project their feelings about themselves onto you. You don't need their approval to live out your dreams, and desperately seeking it is hazardous to your growth.

Anyone who ever accomplished anything great first seemed crazy. Disregard the voices of those who try to keep you mediocre, and stick with the people in your life who know they don't have to fully understand your vision in order to be supportive.

YOUR ACTIONS
HAVE CONSEQUENCES

For every action, there is a reaction. Whatever you do affects what happens next in your life. Whenever you make a poor decision, you have to live with the consequences. You're not entitled to a free pass, nor should you expect people to have sympathy for you because of the choices you've made.

Learn to say you're sorry when you've made a mistake. Take ownership of your behavior and look for ways to right your wrongs. Don't sit back feeling sorry for yourself or blame other people for what you've done; hold yourself accountable. Know that just because someone forgives you, it doesn't mean things automatically go back to how they were in the beginning or that they owe you a spot back in their life. Live wisely, thinking about what can come from your actions, because some consequences are forever.

LET GO OF WHAT'S OUTSIDE OF YOU

Some things will happen to you that are outside of your control. It's easy to automatically react to those things, creating stress, worry, anxiety, or other negative emotions. You will find freedom when you take responsibility for what is within your control and nothing else.

When faced with hard situations, ask yourself: *Is this related to something within my ability to change, or is this outside of me?* If you can do something about a situation, do it. But if you can't, let it go. The energy you expend to take ownership of things that don't belong to you is energy wasted. You can only change what is within yourself, never what is within someone or something else.

LESSON 84

WHATEVER YOU USE TO GET IT IS WHAT YOU WILL NEED TO KEEP IT

I once knew a man who used his material possessions to get women's attention. He'd flaunt his money, cars, jewelry, and fancy clothes to entice the kind of women he (thought) he wanted to date. Once he had captivated them with all of his stuff, he started noticing that the women always wanted more stuff. He grew tired of having to pour out money for things when he wanted to show his true self and be accepted for who he really was inside. The money, cars, and clothes were just supposed to attract the women, much like something shiny on the ground grabs the eyes of a passersby. He didn't realize the women he was pursuing were expecting what he lured them in with. The minute he stopped being so flashy, the women left. To keep those women, he would have needed to keep up with how he got them.

Whatever you use to get something is what you will need to keep it. If you land a job because of your intense work ethic, don't be surprised when your boss starts to question you when you start getting complacent and stop working as hard as you used to. Trouble arises when you can't maintain the standard you portray. This is why it's critical to be yourself from the beginning. It is easier to be the person you genuinely are than to try to uphold the façade of the person you think you should be. If you wear a mask, then the minute you remove your mask, no one will recognize you. There will always be room to grow and improve, but life is less receptive to the dwindling of what you initially claimed to be. This is not an excuse to aim low or give less than your best, but it is a reminder to always be your true self from the start.

LESSON 85

PEOPLE WILL CRITICIZE YOU UNTIL THEY NEED FROM YOU THAT WHICH THEY HAVE CRITICIZED

Regardless of what you do in life, someone will always have something to say about it. Criticism is unavoidable, so don't take it to heart or let it get you down. Check yourself to make sure you aren't confusing advice or feedback for criticism, and then grow from what's honest and constructive. Pay no attention to the rest. Don't be surprised when the people who criticize you the most come back around and start asking you for favors. These people openly express their disapproval of a thing until they suspect they can benefit from it.

Critics will put you down for being too emotional until they need someone to genuinely care for them; that's when they'll come running. They'll criticize you for being too strong willed or assertive until they need someone to fight a literal or figurative battle for them. They'll talk about you for living unconventionally, but then they'll ask how you did it or ask to use the resources you've established for yourself. Whatever they're saying, your critics will only be your critics until they decide they want to be your beneficiaries.

LESSON 86

PRETEND IT'S ALL FUN MONEY

I hope you will experience a life where your income is made doing something you truly love. The likelihood though, is that before you get there, you will work to make money doing something that isn't your favorite job in the world. It can be draining, trying to power through long work days when you're working a job you dislike.

One of the best pieces of advice I've been given about making it through working a job that's more likely to be seen in your nightmares than in your dreams was given to me when I worked as a waitress at a diner in San Francisco. I hated that job; I had terrible hours and a terrible uniform, and I was mistreated by customers on a daily basis. The catch for me was that the money was "good"; my paychecks were high, but so was the cost of living.

Most days were dreadful; working a job I despised for money that went straight to the bills left me frustrated and unfulfilled. It would seem that the obvious solution would have been to just find a better job, but sometimes life isn't always that simple. Sometimes you need something small to get you through the daily grind while you're trying to figure out how to make bigger changes.

One night, in between tears of defeat, I was advised to pretend that all of the money I earned was "fun money." Fun money is money you get to spend any way you choose, without regard to responsibilities. Imagine if you never had to pay a single bill for the rest of your life. What would you spend your money on? You'd be surprised how much more motivating it is to get your work done if the reward at the end is a vacation, your favorite meal, or new clothes, instead of handing over your money for the electric bill.

Even if it's just a thought, sometimes the thought is enough to get you through. So if you find yourself in a work funk you can't shake, pretend it's all fun money.

BALANCE IS BOTH THE MOST IMPORTANT AND THE MOST DIFFICULT

The most important things are also the most difficult to achieve at times. Balance, the art of giving and taking just the right amounts in just the right areas at just the right time, requires careful attention and honest assessment. It calls for us to look at our lives, determine where we're off kilter, and make adjustments where needed. The goal of balance isn't to do everything perfectly all of the time, but to avoid losing yourself in any one thing.

Anything you do has an opposite that is also essential to your overall wellbeing. Both are needed to avoid burnout and feelings of emptiness. If you're always working, your work needs to be balanced with time to play, and if you're always playing, you must balance that with some sort of work. If you spend time with only one person, make time to spend alone or with other important people in your life; this is especially true when you first start dating someone new and every moment is spent obsessing over him, or when you have kids and you get zero time to yourself. If you're always running around, working out, or just being physically active, your body needs to be balanced with rest.

You'll know when your life is out of balance—you'll feel it. It'll feel like something's missing or like you aren't fully yourself. When you notice that one side of your life scale is completely dominating the other, add a little something to the other side. Your scales will never be perfectly balanced, but the closer you get, the healthier your life will be.

YOU CAN BE ANYTHING YOU WANT TO BE EXCEPT A PERSON WHO KEEPS OTHER PEOPLE FROM BEING WHO THEY WANT TO BE

You have the right to decide who and what you want to be in life. If you want to behave a certain way, that's up to you. You get to choose which morals and values you live by, and what qualities you want to express through your personality. Your actions are totally up to you. What isn't up to you is how other people want to live. Just as you have the right to decide, so do they.

Relationships of any kind require compromise. Some days you will receive, and some days you will give. Neither you nor anyone else is obligated to give up a sense of self. The things you value should not be discounted just because someone else doesn't equally value them. If I value punctuality and you don't, and we're going somewhere together, you have every right to be as late as you want to be. You just don't have the right to make me late. You have every right to value your reputation, but you don't have the right to expect me to devalue mine in order to validate yours. We each have the right to uphold our own identity.

Each person also has the right to create and execute boundaries as to how much they're willing to compromise in the relationships they value. Here's an example: If I'm in a relationship and my significant other decides to stop eating meat, he has every right to do that. He does not have the right to demand that I do the same. A compromise in this situation might be that I don't expect him to buy or cook meat, or that I'm willing to go without meat a few times a week so we can enjoy the same meal. Healthy compromises honor the person you love while still honoring yourself. Some relationships can exist harmoniously even if there are differences; whereas, others cannot. If I notice that my significant other is prejudiced and I'm not, I should be unwilling to make compromises to uphold that relationship, even if that means the relationship will cease to exist. Sometimes, choosing what's right to you will cost you, and you'll have to decide what's most important.

Be who you are, while remembering that others have the right to do the same. Know that discrepancies in beliefs may result in your doing certain things alone, and you have to be secure enough in yourself to handle that. Compromise when it makes sense or results in positive growth, but don't give up who you are for others, or expect that others give up who they are for you.

LEARN SOMETHING NEW EVERY DAY

Invest in yourself by making your intellectual growth a daily priority. So many ways exist to obtain knowledge that you have no real excuse not to access the wealth of information available in the world.

Listen to a podcast, a seminar, or a new song. Read a blog, a book, an article, or even a new quote. Visit a new place or an old friend. Enroll in a class. Try something new, or learn from someone else's experiences. Observe the outside world by being still and seeing how things naturally unfold.

Whether you prefer to have generalized or specialized knowledge, focus on learning at least one new thing a day.

DON'T LET PEOPLE WHO ARE CONFUSED ABOUT THEMSELVES MAKE YOU CONFUSED ABOUT YOURSELF

It's one thing to be sure of yourself. It's another thing to be sure of yourself among people who are unsure of themselves. Confused people, intentionally or not, want you to feel uncertain of who you are and what you stand for. Your security forces them to face the fact they believe themselves to be lacking in some areas. That's their battle to fight, not yours.

People who are deeply insecure will try to manipulate you into feeling like maybe the things you know about yourself are wrong. They will project their feelings about themselves onto you and try to pull you down to match their level of misery and confusion. These people will look for the negative in every good thing you try to do, and they will use twisted logic to justify themselves.

Know yourself confidently, and don't let a confused person make you confused too.

LESSON 91

CONSISTENCY IS KEY

If you want to be good at anything or improve anything, you don't have to be perfect, just consistent. Whatever the work is, you just have to continue to do it. You may not be confident yet or even be good at what you're working on, but regularly committing to it will ensure you get better at it. Be disciplined enough to put in the time and effort when you don't see immediate results or when you can't yet see the finish line. Consistency is the key to progress; but the key to consistency is to never stop altogether, even if you have to slow down or take an occasional break.

GO SEE THE WORLD

No matter where you're from or where you're at, it's small in relation to the size of the world. So get out there and see it. Traveling expands your knowledge, perspective, and appreciation. It teaches you not everyone does things the way you do, and it deepens your sense of curiosity, creativity, and empathy. What you can learn from experiencing the world first hand far exceeds anything you can read in a book or watch on your social media feed. Pick a place you want to go, do your research, and begin to execute a plan to get there.

If you can't arrange to leave the country, then travel to a different state, city, or town. If you can't travel by plane, go by ship, bus, car, bike, or on foot if you have to. Just get out of your bubble of familiarity. If money is an issue, start saving now. Use apps that tell you the best time to spend on travel arrangements. Use sites that bundle prices so you can get a discount. Go on a mission trip that allows you to trade volunteer work for travel accommodations. Travel during the middle of the week or go during the off season. Stay for a shorter time, or go somewhere closer.

Stop buying dumb stuff and start investing in lifelong memories. You will get more out of traveling than you'll ever get out of new clothes or that $5 cup of coffee you buy every day. The money, time, and energy spent seeing the world is a small tradeoff for the richness in love, culture, and experience you will gain.

DON'T ALLOW GRATITUDE TO MAKE YOU COMPLACENT

Reminders to practice gratitude have become excessively trendy. Quotes about being grateful can be found on home decor, notebooks, t-shirts, and on city murals. Gratitude is beautiful and transformative, but it's also tricky. Without introspection, we can be feeling guilty or hopeless and pass it off as gratitude.

Some people hate their job but tell themselves they shouldn't strive for more because at least they have a job. This mixture of gratitude and guilt can potentially keep them from pursuing the thing they're destined to do. Are they actually grateful? Or are they just telling themselves they should be grateful, as a way to cover their feeling bad for wanting more when they've already been given much? Some people stay in abusive relationships because they've convinced themselves they should just be grateful for the good times or grateful not to be alone. This isn't gratitude, it's settling. They aren't grateful for abuse; they may just feel they have no other options, so they call it gratitude as a way not to address their hopelessness. If they can convince themselves they're grateful, they can opt out of having to face the unknown.

Gratitude is essential to a fulfilled life, but only if it's genuine. Gratitude should bring you contentment, not complacency. Contentment reflects your ability to find and make happiness wherever you are; being complacent reflects an unwillingness to make changes even if you know you should. Only you know what's actually behind your gratitude. Live a life filled with honest gratitude, but don't use it as a way to cover how you really feel.

LESSON 94

THE PROBLEM MIGHT BE YOU

If everyone around you has the same thoughts and feelings about you, it probably has more to do with you than it does with them. We're happy to accept this idea if everyone thinks we're great, but we'd rather believe that everyone else is the problem if there's a collective negative consensus about us. The opinions of others aren't always accurate, but it's a good rule of thumb that if the people around you all feel the same negative way about you or something you do, the problem is probably you.

Now before you get defensive, first ask yourself: *Do I care what the people in my life think?* If you don't, then feel free to stop reading right here. But if you do care about the possibility that you could be negatively affecting people who matter to you, read on to figure out if you're the problem, and for advice on what to do if you discover that you are.

Start by considering the source. The only voices you should really be taking into consideration are those of people you know, trust, and respect. Listening to every voice is too overwhelming and leaves room for you to be manipulated by people who don't have your best interest at heart. Once you've determined which voices matter, listen to their common expression and then step outside yourself and see if it's true. If everyone in your circle agrees that you have a bad temper, pay attention to how you behave when you're mad. Make an extra effort to see things from their perspective. Remember, if ten out of ten of your loved ones say your temper is scary, that means your temper is scary and you need to do something about it. The idea that everyone should deal with you because "This is just how you are" is played out. People don't have to endure poor treatment, just because you refuse to face your bad behavior. Either fix what you're doing wrong, or be prepared for your relationships to suffer or dissipate altogether.

Tread carefully to ensure that you aren't assuming that people feel a certain way about you. "Everyone thinks I'm a bad person" is different from when your kin all agree it's kind of off-putting that you make yourself the center of every story. This isn't about your emotions or insecurities; it's about facing facts and growing to a higher version of yourself.

If you can't maintain friendships or relationships, the problem is probably you. If no one in your family trusts you, the problem is probably you. If you're always into some kind of trouble, the problem is probably you. Before you get off thinking that the whole world is against you, be open to the possibility that the problem might just be you.

LEAVE IT BETTER
THAN YOU FOUND IT

When I was a kid, if my dad needed a few dollars in cash, he would ask to borrow it from me to avoid going to the bank for a small amount of money. I loved when he asked to borrow money because he would always give me extra when he paid me back. He would say that if you borrowed money from the bank, you'd have to pay interest, so he was paying interest to me. Throughout my life, my parents have been continuous examples of this kind of accountability and integrity. When I got older and my parents would visit me while I was living out of town, my mom never failed to do things I needed without my ever asking. She would clean the things I hated to clean or replace things she noticed were running low. My apartment was always better after my parents had been there.

Your parents are your first teachers, and mine taught me the significance of leaving things better than you found them. If you borrow money from someone, throw in a couple of extra dollars when you repay them. It doesn't have to be a lot; a few dollars is enough for a cup of coffee or a pastry, and it shows your appreciation for the person who helped you. If someone lends you something to wear, return it washed and folded nicely or on a hanger. If you borrow someone's car, bring it back with more gas than it had in it when you took it. If you stay at someone's house, look for ways to help out. Take out the trash or do a load of dishes, and always make up your sleeping space. In your engagements with other people, leave them better than you found them, too. Listen to them, give them a reason to smile, or simply be kind. Add value to the world around you by making the effort to give more than what's expected.

TAKE ADVANTAGE OF INSPIRED MOMENTS

When you feel inspired to do something, act on that inspiration—don't let it pass you by. Don't procrastinate or second-guess yourself. Don't think the inspiration will feel the same at a later time; its unlikely it will.

When you are compelled to do something, do it. That energy will give you momentum, and you will need that momentum to give you a boost when you're lacking motivation. Don't let the inspired moments fizzle out—the fire you feel is meant to light the way.

If you feel like you want to work out, get up and work out. If you feel moved to help someone, do it. If you get an inspired thought, take some kind of action with it. You may not lose that fiery inspiration entirely, but it will never be the same as it was in the moment when you first felt it.

RESPECT YOUR OWN EVOLUTION

In nature, what doesn't evolve, dies. While you probably won't physically die if you don't grow, you will kill off the version of yourself that's needed to expand and progress into your future. It's not only necessary that you grow, it's intended.

You don't have to be the same person you were last year, last month, or last week. It's okay to change. Holding on to old mindsets that no longer serve you will keep you from adopting new ways of thinking that match who you are today. Don't be afraid to let go of the past.

Have patience with yourself as you grow. The pace at which you grow and learn is uniquely yours. You are on your own schedule, so don't try to force or rush your evolution.

Some people don't want to grow. They are too afraid to face who they are in the present, so they prefer to live in the past. Sometimes those people are people you deeply care for, and growing without them can feel like you're leaving them behind. Don't stunt your growth by waiting for others to grow. Growing at different paces is to be expected, but purposely remaining stagnant ultimately benefits no one.

You were designed with evolution in mind; you aren't meant to spend your whole life being the same. Getting to the next level will always require a more refined you. Strive for greatness and embrace who you are becoming.

LIFE IS FULL OF CONTRADICTIONS

What you need to learn or practice in one moment may not be what you need to learn or practice in the next. What's required of you depends on what part of your life journey you're on. At different times, you will be required to be firm or flexible, gentle or strong, present in the now or proactive towards the future. You will be required to practice contradictory behaviors, and the contradictions won't always make sense. That's when you will have to tune in to discernment, to know when to exercise what. You may not always get it right, but the way to get it wrong is to assume that what works in one situation will be what works in all situations.

Just because you learn in one aspect that not every negative characteristic you have is your fault, doesn't mean you aren't the problem in another. Just because you are encouraged not to hesitate or procrastinate doesn't mean you should make decisions without thinking them through. Just because you think or behave one way in one setting and adjust accordingly in another doesn't make you a hypocrite; it makes you a person who knows that some contradictions are part of a preconceived plan for the development of your character.

NO ONE CAN TELL YOU HOW

Reading through this book, you will find few *how-tos* interwoven into the lessons. This is intentional.

Life is complex. Some things can be taught, while others must be experienced. I can offer my guidance by sharing what has and has not worked for me, but there is never one single right way to do anything. My *how* may be different from the next person's, and that person's *how* may be different from the *how* that works for you. *How* is part of your self-discovery, and only you can be in charge of that.

LESSON 100

MY LOVE FOR YOU
KNOWS NO BOUNDS

If I could have only one conversation with you, I would want it to start and end with love. The stuff in the middle is important, but love is the most important. You act differently when you know you're loved. You take on the world differently when you know you're loved. Above all, you see yourself differently when you know you're loved, and how you see yourself affects how you see everything else. If you take nothing else from what I've shared, I hope you will take this: You are unconditionally loved, you are valuable beyond measure, and you are your Creator's greatest creation.

I hope you will fully experience all of your good days; and on your hard days, I hope you will remember trouble is temporary and your life is worth living. Whatever gets thrown your way, I hope you will always know how capable you are. I hope you will go forth with confidence, trusting that you are never too far out of love's reach.

You are, in your essence, a gift to the world, designed with purpose and intention, and I pray you never forget that.

All my love.

ABOUT THE AUTHOR

Alexis Chanyl has been writing since she was eight years old. But it took losing her unborn child to miscarriage to inspire her to write her first book, *For Mercy: Lessons I Would Have Taught My Daughter.* Seeking to share her story, connect with other women and express the powerful love she felt for the little girl she never knew, she compiled 100 "lessons" ranging from things she wished someone taught her when she was younger to ways to help any woman feel better about herself, expand her mind, or feel inspired and empowered to give more to the world.

A graduate of California State University Long Beach with a degree in psychology, Chanyl became fascinated with the differences in how men and women are socialized. The book reflects her passion for helping women achieve their full potential by working together and supporting each other. She currently runs a women's empowerment group called "SisterShares" with her younger sister, and penned *For Mercy,* "as much as an act of sisterhood as it is in motherhood" for anyone looking to connect and grow.

Chanyl is a native of the Golden State and still lives and writes in Southern California. Her other passions include spoken word poetry, her 9-year-old son, and seeking out adventure and new experiences wherever she can find them.

For Mercy is Chanyl's first book.

You can connect with her on Instagram @AlexisChanyl.

Made in the USA
Middletown, DE
22 October 2021

50749977R00076